**TEACHER'S PET PUBLICATIONS**

PUZZLE PACK
for
The Cay
based on the book by
Theodore Taylor

Written by
William T. Collins

© 2005 Teacher's Pet Publications
All Rights Reserved

The materials in this packet are copyrighted
by Teacher's Pet Publications, Inc.

These pages may be duplicated by the purchaser
for use in the purchaser's own classroom.

Copying any of these materials and distributing them
for any other purpose is a violation of the copyright laws.

© 2005 Teacher's Pet Publications, Inc.
www.tpet.com

INTRODUCTION
If you already own the LitPlan for this title, this Puzzle Pack will refresh your Unit Resource Materials and Vocabulary Resource Materials sections plus give you additional materials you can substitute into the tests. If you do not already have a complete LitPlan, these pages will give you some supplemental materials to use with your own plan. There are two main groups of materials: one set for unit words (such as characters' names, symbols, places, etc.) and one set for vocabulary words associated with the book.

WORD LIST
There is a word list for both the unit words and the vocabulary words. These lists show you which words are being used in the materials and the clues or definitions being used for those words. You may want to give students a word list with clues/definitions to help them, or you may want students to only have a word list (without clues/definitions) if you want them to work a little harder. Both are available for duplication. The word lists can also be your "calling key" for the bingo games.

FILL IN THE BLANK AND MATCHING
There are 4 each of the fill in the blank and matching worksheets for both the unit and vocabulary words. These pages can be used either as extra worksheets for students or as objective parts of a unit test. They can be done individually if students need extra help or as a whole class activity to review the material covered.

MAGIC SQUARES
The magic squares not only reinforce the material covered but also work on reasoning and math skills. Many teachers have told us that their students really enjoy doing these!

WORD SEARCH PUZZLES
The word search words go in all directions, as indicated on your answer keys. Two of the word search puzzles have the clues listed rather than the words. This makes the puzzle a little more difficult, but it reinforces the material better. Two word search puzzles have words only for students who find the clue puzzles too difficult.

CROSSWORD PUZZLES
Both unit and vocabulary word sections have 4 crossword puzzles.

BINGO CARDS
There are 32 individual bingo cards for the unit words and 32 individual bingo cards for the vocabulary words. You can use your word list as a "call list," calling the words at random and marking them off of your list as you go, or you could use the flash cards by cutting them apart and drawing the words at random from a hat (or box or whatever). To make a better review, you might ask for the definition and spelling of each word as you call it out–or you could call out the definitions and have students tell you the words they need to look for on the puzzle.

JUGGLE LETTERS
The vocabulary juggle letter game is intended to help students learn the spellings of the words. One sheet has the definitions listed on it as an extra help for students who need it or to reinforce the definitions if you choose to do so.

FLASH CARDS
We've included a set of vocabulary flash cards you can duplicate, cut, and fold for your students. Some teachers make a few sets for general use by the class; others make a set for each student. Some teachers duplicate them for each student and have the students cut & fold their own. You can cut out just the words and put them in a hat, have each student pick out one word and write the definition and a sentence for that word. Students then swap words and papers, with the next student adding a sentence of his own under the last one. You can have students swap as many times as you like. Each time the student will read the sentences written prior to his own and then add a sentence. You can cut out the words and definitions separately and play "I Have; Who Has?" Each student in the room draws a word and definition. The first student says, "I have (the name of the word). Who has the definition?" The student with the definition reads it then says, "I have (the name of the vocabulary word she has). Who has the definition?" The round continues until all words and definitions have been given.

The Cay Word List

No.	Word	Clue/Definition
1.	AMERICAN	Nationality of Phillip and Timothy
2.	BAD	The cat was ___ luck.
3.	BAHSS	Timothy called Phillip Young ___.
4.	BELL	Sound that alerted Phillip his rescuers were coming
5.	BIRDS	They attacked Phillip.
6.	BLIND	Phillip lost his sight. He was ___.
7.	BRIDGE	Queen Emma was a ____
8.	CAN	They put a pebble in it each day.
9.	CONFLICT	Man vs. Nature, for example
10.	CORAL	It made navigating around the cays difficult.
11.	CURACAO	Place where Mr. Enright was sent to work
12.	DEVIL	____'s Mouth; name of the area of the cays
13.	ENRIGHT	Phillip's last name
14.	FISH	Phillip learned to do this to feed himself.
15.	GRAPE	Phillip used these oily leaves to make black smoke.
16.	HATO	Ship Phillip & his mother took towards Miami
17.	HELP	Word they spelled on the beach in stones
18.	HENRIK	Phillip's Dutch friend
19.	HUT	It was blown away.
20.	JULY	Month the hurricane hit
21.	JUMBI	Evil spirit
22.	KEG	They lashed the water ___ to a tree trunk.
23.	LANGOSTAS	Clawless lobsters Timothy caught for food
24.	MALARIA	Illness that struck Timothy
25.	MATS	Timothy asked Phillip to weave sleeping _____.
26.	MELON	Shape of the island
27.	MOTHER	I wouldn't even be here with you if it wasn't for my ____.
28.	NAZIS	They sent U-boats to destroy ships.
29.	PHILLIP	He regained his sight after operations.
30.	RAFT	It carried Timothy, Phillip & the cat
31.	REFINERY	Where Mr. Enright worked
32.	ROPE	Timothy made this with vines for Phillip.
33.	SEVENTY	Timothy was over ___ years old.
34.	SHARKS	Phillip fell off the raft into the water with _____.
35.	STEW	Name of the cook's cat
36.	SUN	Phillip covered Timothy in grape leaves to protect him from the ____.
37.	TANKERS	The Chinese crews on the ___ refused to sail.
38.	TAYLOR	Author Theodore
39.	TERN	After the sinking of the ___, Phillip began to understand that war meant death and destruction.
40.	THOMAS	Timothy's home was on St. ____
41.	TIMOTHY	Negro man who cared for Phillip
42.	TORPEDOED	The Hato was ___ on April 6, 1942.
43.	TREE	At first Phillip was too afraid to climb it.
44.	VIRGINIA	The Enrights were from this US state.
45.	WATER	Timothy & Phillip each had 1/2 cup of it to celebrate landfall.

The Cay Unit Fill In The Blank 1

_____ 1. After the sinking of the ___, Phillip began to understand that war meant death and destruction.

_____ 2. Phillip's last name

_____ 3. I wouldn't even be here with you if it wasn't for my ____.

_____ 4. He regained his sight after operations.

_____ 5. At first Phillip was too afraid to climb it.

_____ 6. Negro man who cared for Phillip

_____ 7. Shape of the island

_____ 8. Phillip used these oily leaves to make black smoke.

_____ 9. Phillip fell off the raft into the water with _____.

_____ 10. Timothy was over ___ years old.

_____ 11. The Enrights were from this US state.

_____ 12. It made navigating around the cays difficult.

_____ 13. They put a pebble in it each day.

_____ 14. Clawless lobsters Timothy caught for food

_____ 15. It was blown away.

_____ 16. Phillip covered Timothy in grape leaves to protect him from the ____.

_____ 17. They lashed the water ___ to a tree trunk.

_____ 18. Author Theodore

_____ 19. Word they spelled on the beach in stones

_____ 20. Where Mr. Enright worked

The Cay Unit Fill In The Blank 1 Answer Key

TERN	1. After the sinking of the ___, Phillip began to understand that war meant death and destruction.
ENRIGHT	2. Phillip's last name
MOTHER	3. I wouldn't even be here with you if it wasn't for my ____.
PHILLIP	4. He regained his sight after operations.
TREE	5. At first Phillip was too afraid to climb it.
TIMOTHY	6. Negro man who cared for Phillip
MELON	7. Shape of the island
GRAPE	8. Phillip used these oily leaves to make black smoke.
SHARKS	9. Phillip fell off the raft into the water with _____.
SEVENTY	10. Timothy was over ___ years old.
VIRGINIA	11. The Enrights were from this US state.
CORAL	12. It made navigating around the cays difficult.
CAN	13. They put a pebble in it each day.
LANGOSTAS	14. Clawless lobsters Timothy caught for food
HUT	15. It was blown away.
SUN	16. Phillip covered Timothy in grape leaves to protect him from the ____.
KEG	17. They lashed the water ___ to a tree trunk.
TAYLOR	18. Author Theodore
HELP	19. Word they spelled on the beach in stones
REFINERY	20. Where Mr. Enright worked

The Cay Unit Fill In The Blank 2

_____ 1. The Enrights were from this US state.

_____ 2. Evil spirit

_____ 3. Place where Mr. Enright was sent to work

_____ 4. Timothy & Phillip each had 1/2 cup of it to celebrate landfall.

_____ 5. Phillip's last name

_____ 6. Queen Emma was a ____

_____ 7. Phillip fell off the raft into the water with _____.

_____ 8. At first Phillip was too afraid to climb it.

_____ 9. They attacked Phillip.

_____ 10. Illness that struck Timothy

_____ 11. They put a pebble in it each day.

_____ 12. Nationality of Phillip and Timothy

_____ 13. Word they spelled on the beach in stones

_____ 14. Timothy was over ___ years old.

_____ 15. The Hato was ___ on April 6, 1942.

_____ 16. They sent U-boats to destroy ships.

_____ 17. The Chinese crews on the ___ refused to sail.

_____ 18. Timothy made this with vines for Phillip.

_____ 19. It was blown away.

_____ 20. Ship Phillip & his mother took towards Miami

The Cay Unit Fill In The Blank 2 Answer Key

VIRGINIA	1. The Enrights were from this US state.
JUMBI	2. Evil spirit
CURACAO	3. Place where Mr. Enright was sent to work
WATER	4. Timothy & Phillip each had 1/2 cup of it to celebrate landfall.
ENRIGHT	5. Phillip's last name
BRIDGE	6. Queen Emma was a ____
SHARKS	7. Phillip fell off the raft into the water with ____.
TREE	8. At first Phillip was too afraid to climb it.
BIRDS	9. They attacked Phillip.
MALARIA	10. Illness that struck Timothy
CAN	11. They put a pebble in it each day.
AMERICAN	12. Nationality of Phillip and Timothy
HELP	13. Word they spelled on the beach in stones
SEVENTY	14. Timothy was over ___ years old.
TORPEDOED	15. The Hato was ___ on April 6, 1942.
NAZIS	16. They sent U-boats to destroy ships.
TANKERS	17. The Chinese crews on the ___ refused to sail.
ROPE	18. Timothy made this with vines for Phillip.
HUT	19. It was blown away.
HATO	20. Ship Phillip & his mother took towards Miami

Copyrighted

The Cay Unit Fill In The Blank 3

_____

1. Illness that struck Timothy
2. ____'s Mouth; name of the area of the cays
3. They lashed the water ___ to a tree trunk.
4. Timothy called Phillip Young ___.
5. Ship Phillip & his mother took towards Miami
6. Clawless lobsters Timothy caught for food
7. Phillip lost his sight. He was ___.
8. Phillip fell off the raft into the water with _____.
9. At first Phillip was too afraid to climb it.
10. Timothy made this with vines for Phillip.
11. He regained his sight after operations.
12. The cat was ___ luck.
13. Where Mr. Enright worked
14. Queen Emma was a ____
15. Phillip covered Timothy in grape leaves to protect him from the ____.
16. Phillip used these oily leaves to make black smoke.
17. Month the hurricane hit
18. Phillip learned to do this to feed himself.
19. Man vs. Nature, for example
20. Phillip's Dutch friend

The Cay Unit Fill In The Blank 3 Answer Key

MALARIA	1. Illness that struck Timothy
DEVIL	2. ____'s Mouth; name of the area of the cays
KEG	3. They lashed the water ___ to a tree trunk.
BAHSS	4. Timothy called Phillip Young ___.
HATO	5. Ship Phillip & his mother took towards Miami
LANGOSTAS	6. Clawless lobsters Timothy caught for food
BLIND	7. Phillip lost his sight. He was ___.
SHARKS	8. Phillip fell off the raft into the water with _____.
TREE	9. At first Phillip was too afraid to climb it.
ROPE	10. Timothy made this with vines for Phillip.
PHILLIP	11. He regained his sight after operations.
BAD	12. The cat was ___ luck.
REFINERY	13. Where Mr. Enright worked
BRIDGE	14. Queen Emma was a ____
SUN	15. Phillip covered Timothy in grape leaves to protect him from the ____.
GRAPE	16. Phillip used these oily leaves to make black smoke.
JULY	17. Month the hurricane hit
FISH	18. Phillip learned to do this to feed himself.
CONFLICT	19. Man vs. Nature, for example
HENRIK	20. Phillip's Dutch friend

The Cay Unit Fill In The Blank 4

_____ 1. Word they spelled on the beach in stones

_____ 2. Phillip's last name

_____ 3. Nationality of Phillip and Timothy

_____ 4. Shape of the island

_____ 5. They lashed the water ___ to a tree trunk.

_____ 6. Phillip learned to do this to feed himself.

_____ 7. Name of the cook's cat

_____ 8. After the sinking of the ___, Phillip began to understand that war meant death and destruction.

_____ 9. Phillip lost his sight. He was ___.

_____ 10. Timothy made this with vines for Phillip.

_____ 11. Phillip's Dutch friend

_____ 12. Where Mr. Enright worked

_____ 13. Clawless lobsters Timothy caught for food

_____ 14. It made navigating around the cays difficult.

_____ 15. The Chinese crews on the ___ refused to sail.

_____ 16. The Enrights were from this US state.

_____ 17. Place where Mr. Enright was sent to work

_____ 18. Phillip fell off the raft into the water with _____.

_____ 19. They sent U-boats to destroy ships.

_____ 20. Ship Phillip & his mother took towards Miami

The Cay Unit Fill In The Blank 4 Answer Key

HELP	1. Word they spelled on the beach in stones
ENRIGHT	2. Phillip's last name
AMERICAN	3. Nationality of Phillip and Timothy
MELON	4. Shape of the island
KEG	5. They lashed the water ___ to a tree trunk.
FISH	6. Phillip learned to do this to feed himself.
STEW	7. Name of the cook's cat
TERN	8. After the sinking of the ___, Phillip began to understand that war meant death and destruction.
BLIND	9. Phillip lost his sight. He was ___.
ROPE	10. Timothy made this with vines for Phillip.
HENRIK	11. Phillip's Dutch friend
REFINERY	12. Where Mr. Enright worked
LANGOSTAS	13. Clawless lobsters Timothy caught for food
CORAL	14. It made navigating around the cays difficult.
TANKERS	15. The Chinese crews on the ___ refused to sail.
VIRGINIA	16. The Enrights were from this US state.
CURACAO	17. Place where Mr. Enright was sent to work
SHARKS	18. Phillip fell off the raft into the water with _____.
NAZIS	19. They sent U-boats to destroy ships.
HATO	20. Ship Phillip & his mother took towards Miami

The Cay Unit Matching 1

___ 1. BAHSS   A. Name of the cook's cat
___ 2. LANGOSTAS   B. The cat was ___ luck.
___ 3. CAN   C. Timothy made this with vines for Phillip.
___ 4. THOMAS   D. Timothy called Phillip Young ___.
___ 5. TIMOTHY   E. Shape of the island
___ 6. BRIDGE   F. Phillip lost his sight. He was ___.
___ 7. DEVIL   G. Clawless lobsters Timothy caught for food
___ 8. HUT   H. Timothy asked Phillip to weave sleeping _____.
___ 9. MELON   I. Negro man who cared for Phillip
___ 10. RAFT   J. Phillip's Dutch friend
___ 11. HENRIK   K. Phillip fell off the raft into the water with _____.
___ 12. BAD   L. ____'s Mouth; name of the area of the cays
___ 13. JULY   M. Queen Emma was a ____
___ 14. SHARKS   N. Phillip used these oily leaves to make black smoke.
___ 15. ENRIGHT   O. Illness that struck Timothy
___ 16. ROPE   P. It carried Timothy, Phillip & the cat
___ 17. SEVENTY   Q. Ship Phillip & his mother took towards Miami
___ 18. HATO   R. Phillip's last name
___ 19. SUN   S. Phillip covered Timothy in grape leaves to protect him from the ____.
___ 20. STEW   T. Timothy & Phillip each had 1/2 cup of it to celebrate landfall.
___ 21. GRAPE   U. Timothy was over ___ years old.
___ 22. BLIND   V. It was blown away.
___ 23. WATER   W. Month the hurricane hit
___ 24. MALARIA   X. Timothy's home was on St. ____
___ 25. MATS   Y. They put a pebble in it each day.

The Cay Unit Matching 1 Answer Key

D - 1.	BAHSS	A. Name of the cook's cat
G - 2.	LANGOSTAS	B. The cat was ___ luck.
Y - 3.	CAN	C. Timothy made this with vines for Phillip.
X - 4.	THOMAS	D. Timothy called Phillip Young ___.
I - 5.	TIMOTHY	E. Shape of the island
M - 6.	BRIDGE	F. Phillip lost his sight. He was ___.
L - 7.	DEVIL	G. Clawless lobsters Timothy caught for food
V - 8.	HUT	H. Timothy asked Phillip to weave sleeping ___.
E - 9.	MELON	I. Negro man who cared for Phillip
P - 10.	RAFT	J. Phillip's Dutch friend
J - 11.	HENRIK	K. Phillip fell off the raft into the water with ___.
B - 12.	BAD	L. ___'s Mouth; name of the area of the cays
W - 13.	JULY	M. Queen Emma was a ___
K - 14.	SHARKS	N. Phillip used these oily leaves to make black smoke.
R - 15.	ENRIGHT	O. Illness that struck Timothy
C - 16.	ROPE	P. It carried Timothy, Phillip & the cat
U - 17.	SEVENTY	Q. Ship Phillip & his mother took towards Miami
Q - 18.	HATO	R. Phillip's last name
S - 19.	SUN	S. Phillip covered Timothy in grape leaves to protect him from the ___.
A - 20.	STEW	T. Timothy & Phillip each had 1/2 cup of it to celebrate landfall.
N - 21.	GRAPE	U. Timothy was over ___ years old.
F - 22.	BLIND	V. It was blown away.
T - 23.	WATER	W. Month the hurricane hit
O - 24.	MALARIA	X. Timothy's home was on St. ___
H - 25.	MATS	Y. They put a pebble in it each day.

The Cay Unit Matching 2

___ 1. STEW   A. Name of the cook's cat
___ 2. SEVENTY   B. Timothy called Phillip Young ___.
___ 3. BAHSS   C. Man vs. Nature, for example
___ 4. HELP   D. Shape of the island
___ 5. SUN   E. They sent U-boats to destroy ships.
___ 6. GRAPE   F. Timothy was over ___ years old.
___ 7. WATER   G. Phillip's Dutch friend
___ 8. BIRDS   H. They attacked Phillip.
___ 9. REFINERY   I. Nationality of Phillip and Timothy
___10. BLIND   J. Timothy asked Phillip to weave sleeping _____.
___11. CURACAO   K. Phillip used these oily leaves to make black smoke.
___12. MATS   L. Timothy & Phillip each had 1/2 cup of it to celebrate landfall.
___13. NAZIS   M. Phillip learned to do this to feed himself.
___14. MELON   N. Word they spelled on the beach in stones
___15. FISH   O. Queen Emma was a _____
___16. LANGOSTAS   P. The Enrights were from this US state.
___17. BELL   Q. After the sinking of the ___, Phillip began to understand that war meant death and destruction.
___18. BRIDGE   R. Place where Mr. Enright was sent to work
___19. CONFLICT   S. It carried Timothy, Phillip & the cat
___20. RAFT   T. Clawless lobsters Timothy caught for food
___21. TERN   U. Phillip covered Timothy in grape leaves to protect him from the _____.
___22. HENRIK   V. They put a pebble in it each day.
___23. AMERICAN   W. Phillip lost his sight. He was ___.
___24. CAN   X. Where Mr. Enright worked
___25. VIRGINIA   Y. Sound that alerted Phillip his rescuers were coming

The Cay Unit Matching 2 Answer Key

A - 1. STEW	A.	Name of the cook's cat
F - 2. SEVENTY	B.	Timothy called Phillip Young ___.
B - 3. BAHSS	C.	Man vs. Nature, for example
N - 4. HELP	D.	Shape of the island
U - 5. SUN	E.	They sent U-boats to destroy ships.
K - 6. GRAPE	F.	Timothy was over ___ years old.
L - 7. WATER	G.	Phillip's Dutch friend
H - 8. BIRDS	H.	They attacked Phillip.
X - 9. REFINERY	I.	Nationality of Phillip and Timothy
W -10. BLIND	J.	Timothy asked Phillip to weave sleeping _____.
R -11. CURACAO	K.	Phillip used these oily leaves to make black smoke.
J -12. MATS	L.	Timothy & Phillip each had 1/2 cup of it to celebrate landfall.
E -13. NAZIS	M.	Phillip learned to do this to feed himself.
D -14. MELON	N.	Word they spelled on the beach in stones
M -15. FISH	O.	Queen Emma was a ____
T -16. LANGOSTAS	P.	The Enrights were from this US state.
Y -17. BELL	Q.	After the sinking of the ___, Phillip began to understand that war meant death and destruction.
O -18. BRIDGE	R.	Place where Mr. Enright was sent to work
C -19. CONFLICT	S.	It carried Timothy, Phillip & the cat
S -20. RAFT	T.	Clawless lobsters Timothy caught for food
Q -21. TERN	U.	Phillip covered Timothy in grape leaves to protect him from the ____.
G -22. HENRIK	V.	They put a pebble in it each day.
I - 23. AMERICAN	W.	Phillip lost his sight. He was ___.
V -24. CAN	X.	Where Mr. Enright worked
P -25. VIRGINIA	Y.	Sound that alerted Phillip his rescuers were coming

The Cay Unit Matching 3

___ 1. TAYLOR   A. Phillip lost his sight. He was ___.
___ 2. BELL   B. Timothy's home was on St. ____
___ 3. THOMAS   C. Clawless lobsters Timothy caught for food
___ 4. TREE   D. It carried Timothy, Phillip & the cat
___ 5. HELP   E. Word they spelled on the beach in stones
___ 6. LANGOSTAS   F. Timothy asked Phillip to weave sleeping _____.
___ 7. HENRIK   G. Phillip's last name
___ 8. HATO   H. He regained his sight after operations.
___ 9. STEW   I. Place where Mr. Enright was sent to work
___ 10. CURACAO   J. At first Phillip was too afraid to climb it.
___ 11. JUMBI   K. Phillip learned to do this to feed himself.
___ 12. MOTHER   L. It made navigating around the cays difficult.
___ 13. NAZIS   M. The Enrights were from this US state.
___ 14. FISH   N. Phillip used these oily leaves to make black smoke.
___ 15. VIRGINIA   O. They sent U-boats to destroy ships.
___ 16. ENRIGHT   P. After the sinking of the ___, Phillip began to understand that war meant death and destruction.
___ 17. BAHSS   Q. Ship Phillip & his mother took towards Miami
___ 18. MATS   R. Timothy was over ___ years old.
___ 19. GRAPE   S. Name of the cook's cat
___ 20. RAFT   T. Evil spirit
___ 21. PHILLIP   U. Sound that alerted Phillip his rescuers were coming
___ 22. BLIND   V. I wouldn't even be here with you if it wasn't for my ____.
___ 23. TERN   W. Phillip's Dutch friend
___ 24. SEVENTY   X. Timothy called Phillip Young ___.
___ 25. CORAL   Y. Author Theodore

The Cay Unit Matcing 3 Answer Key

Y - 1. TAYLOR	A.	Phillip lost his sight. He was ___.
U - 2. BELL	B.	Timothy's home was on St. ___
B - 3. THOMAS	C.	Clawless lobsters Timothy caught for food
J - 4. TREE	D.	It carried Timothy, Phillip & the cat
E - 5. HELP	E.	Word they spelled on the beach in stones
C - 6. LANGOSTAS	F.	Timothy asked Phillip to weave sleeping ___.
W - 7. HENRIK	G.	Phillip's last name
Q - 8. HATO	H.	He regained his sight after operations.
S - 9. STEW	I.	Place where Mr. Enright was sent to work
I - 10. CURACAO	J.	At first Phillip was too afraid to climb it.
T - 11. JUMBI	K.	Phillip learned to do this to feed himself.
V - 12. MOTHER	L.	It made navigating around the cays difficult.
O - 13. NAZIS	M.	The Enrights were from this US state.
K - 14. FISH	N.	Phillip used these oily leaves to make black smoke.
M - 15. VIRGINIA	O.	They sent U-boats to destroy ships.
G - 16. ENRIGHT	P.	After the sinking of the ___, Phillip began to understand that war meant death and destruction.
X - 17. BAHSS	Q.	Ship Phillip & his mother took towards Miami
F - 18. MATS	R.	Timothy was over ___ years old.
N - 19. GRAPE	S.	Name of the cook's cat
D - 20. RAFT	T.	Evil spirit
H - 21. PHILLIP	U.	Sound that alerted Phillip his rescuers were coming
A - 22. BLIND	V.	I wouldn't even be here with you if it wasn't for my ___.
P - 23. TERN	W.	Phillip's Dutch friend
R - 24. SEVENTY	X.	Timothy called Phillip Young ___.
L - 25. CORAL	Y.	Author Theodore

The Cay Unit Matching 4

___ 1. LANGOSTAS   A. Word they spelled on the beach in stones
___ 2. TAYLOR   B. The Hato was ___ on April 6, 1942.
___ 3. MALARIA   C. Timothy & Phillip each had 1/2 cup of it to celebrate landfall.
___ 4. WATER   D. At first Phillip was too afraid to climb it.
___ 5. TIMOTHY   E. They lashed the water ___ to a tree trunk.
___ 6. TREE   F. Shape of the island
___ 7. MATS   G. It carried Timothy, Phillip & the cat
___ 8. PHILLIP   H. Clawless lobsters Timothy caught for food
___ 9. THOMAS   I. I wouldn't even be here with you if it wasn't for my ____.
___ 10. SEVENTY   J. Timothy's home was on St. ____
___ 11. CURACAO   K. Phillip learned to do this to feed himself.
___ 12. KEG   L. Timothy asked Phillip to weave sleeping _____.
___ 13. MELON   M. Man vs. Nature, for example
___ 14. BELL   N. Timothy was over ___ years old.
___ 15. JUMBI   O. Illness that struck Timothy
___ 16. RAFT   P. Place where Mr. Enright was sent to work
___ 17. FISH   Q. He regained his sight after operations.
___ 18. SHARKS   R. Evil spirit
___ 19. TORPEDOED   S. After the sinking of the ___, Phillip began to understand that war meant death and destruction.
___ 20. BAHSS   T. Phillip fell off the raft into the water with _____.
___ 21. BIRDS   U. They attacked Phillip.
___ 22. TERN   V. Sound that alerted Phillip his rescuers were coming
___ 23. CONFLICT   W. Timothy called Phillip Young ___.
___ 24. MOTHER   X. Author Theodore
___ 25. HELP   Y. Negro man who cared for Phillip

The Cay Unit Matching 4 Answer Key

H - 1. LANGOSTAS	A.	Word they spelled on the beach in stones
X - 2. TAYLOR	B.	The Hato was ___ on April 6, 1942.
O - 3. MALARIA	C.	Timothy & Phillip each had 1/2 cup of it to celebrate landfall.
C - 4. WATER	D.	At first Phillip was too afraid to climb it.
Y - 5. TIMOTHY	E.	They lashed the water ___ to a tree trunk.
D - 6. TREE	F.	Shape of the island
L - 7. MATS	G.	It carried Timothy, Phillip & the cat
Q - 8. PHILLIP	H.	Clawless lobsters Timothy caught for food
J - 9. THOMAS	I.	I wouldn't even be here with you if it wasn't for my ___.
N -10. SEVENTY	J.	Timothy's home was on St. ___
P -11. CURACAO	K.	Phillip learned to do this to feed himself.
E -12. KEG	L.	Timothy asked Phillip to weave sleeping ___.
F -13. MELON	M.	Man vs. Nature, for example
V -14. BELL	N.	Timothy was over ___ years old.
R -15. JUMBI	O.	Illness that struck Timothy
G -16. RAFT	P.	Place where Mr. Enright was sent to work
K -17. FISH	Q.	He regained his sight after operations.
T -18. SHARKS	R.	Evil spirit
B -19. TORPEDOED	S.	After the sinking of the ___, Phillip began to understand that war meant death and destruction.
W -20. BAHSS	T.	Phillip fell off the raft into the water with ___.
U -21. BIRDS	U.	They attacked Phillip.
S -22. TERN	V.	Sound that alerted Phillip his rescuers were coming
M -23. CONFLICT	W.	Timothy called Phillip Young ___.
I - 24. MOTHER	X.	Author Theodore
A -25. HELP	Y.	Negro man who cared for Phillip

The Cay Unit Magic Squares 1

Match the definition with the vocabulary word. Put your answers in the magic squares below. When your answers are correct, all columns and rows will add to the same number.

A. CONFLICT   E. REFINERY   I. KEG   M. HATO
B. FISH   F. CAN   J. JULY   N. MOTHER
C. MATS   G. BIRDS   K. GRAPE   O. SUN
D. STEW   H. HENRIK   L. MELON   P. SHARKS

1. Man vs. Nature, for example
2. I wouldn't even be here with you if it wasn't for my ____.
3. Month the hurricane hit
4. Where Mr. Enright worked
5. They attacked Phillip.
6. Shape of the island
7. Phillip fell off the raft into the water with _____.
8. Timothy asked Phillip to weave sleeping _____.
9. Phillip covered Timothy in grape leaves to protect him from the ____.
10. Name of the cook's cat
11. Phillip's Dutch friend
12. Phillip used these oily leaves to make black smoke.
13. They lashed the water ___ to a tree trunk.
14. They put a pebble in it each day.
15. Phillip learned to do this to feed himself.
16. Ship Phillip & his mother took towards Miami

A=	B=	C=	D=
E=	F=	G=	H=
I=	J=	K=	L=
M=	N=	O=	P=

The Cay Unit Magic Squares 1 Answer Key

Match the definition with the vocabulary word. Put your answers in the magic squares below. When your answers are correct, all columns and rows will add to the same number.

A. CONFLICT   E. REFINERY   I. KEG   M. HATO
B. FISH   F. CAN   J. JULY   N. MOTHER
C. MATS   G. BIRDS   K. GRAPE   O. SUN
D. STEW   H. HENRIK   L. MELON   P. SHARKS

1. Man vs. Nature, for example
2. I wouldn't even be here with you if it wasn't for my ____.
3. Month the hurricane hit
4. Where Mr. Enright worked
5. They attacked Phillip.
6. Shape of the island
7. Phillip fell off the raft into the water with _____.
8. Timothy asked Phillip to weave sleeping _____.
9. Phillip covered Timothy in grape leaves to protect him from the ____.
10. Name of the cook's cat
11. Phillip's Dutch friend
12. Phillip used these oily leaves to make black smoke.
13. They lashed the water ___ to a tree trunk.
14. They put a pebble in it each day.
15. Phillip learned to do this to feed himself.
16. Ship Phillip & his mother took towards Miami

A=1	B=15	C=8	D=10
E=4	F=14	G=5	H=11
I=13	J=3	K=12	L=6
M=16	N=2	O=9	P=7

Copyrighted

The Cay Unit Magic Squares 2

Match the definition with the vocabulary word. Put your answers in the magic squares below. When your answers are correct, all columns and rows will add to the same number.

A. TERN
B. CONFLICT
C. DEVIL
D. MOTHER
E. STEW
F. HELP
G. CORAL
H. TANKERS
I. THOMAS
J. HENRIK
K. NAZIS
L. CURACAO
M. TORPEDOED
N. TAYLOR
O. SHARKS
P. PHILLIP

1. The Chinese crews on the ___ refused to sail.
2. The Hato was ___ on April 6, 1942.
3. Man vs. Nature, for example
4. They sent U-boats to destroy ships.
5. Phillip's Dutch friend
6. ____'s Mouth; name of the area of the cays
7. He regained his sight after operations.
8. Name of the cook's cat
9. Phillip fell off the raft into the water with ____.
10. Word they spelled on the beach in stones
11. Timothy's home was on St. ____
12. I wouldn't even be here with you if it wasn't for my ____.
13. After the sinking of the ___, Phillip began to understand that war meant death and destruction.
14. Place where Mr. Enright was sent to work
15. It made navigating around the cays difficult.
16. Author Theodore

A=	B=	C=	D=
E=	F=	G=	H=
I=	J=	K=	L=
M=	N=	O=	P=

23
Copyrighted

The Cay Unit Magic Squares 2 Answer Key

Match the definition with the vocabulary word. Put your answers in the magic squares below. When your answers are correct, all columns and rows will add to the same number.

A. TERN   E. STEW   I. THOMAS   M. TORPEDOED
B. CONFLICT   F. HELP   J. HENRIK   N. TAYLOR
C. DEVIL   G. CORAL   K. NAZIS   O. SHARKS
D. MOTHER   H. TANKERS   L. CURACAO   P. PHILLIP

1. The Chinese crews on the ___ refused to sail.
2. The Hato was ___ on April 6, 1942.
3. Man vs. Nature, for example
4. They sent U-boats to destroy ships.
5. Phillip's Dutch friend
6. ____'s Mouth; name of the area of the cays
7. He regained his sight after operations.
8. Name of the cook's cat
9. Phillip fell off the raft into the water with _____.
10. Word they spelled on the beach in stones
11. Timothy's home was on St. ____
12. I wouldn't even be here with you if it wasn't for my ____.
13. After the sinking of the ___, Phillip began to understand that war meant death and destruction.
14. Place where Mr. Enright was sent to work
15. It made navigating around the cays difficult.
16. Author Theodore

A=13	B=3	C=6	D=12
E=8	F=10	G=15	H=1
I=11	J=5	K=4	L=14
M=2	N=16	O=9	P=7

The Cay Unit Magic Squares 3

Match the definition with the vocabulary word. Put your answers in the magic squares below. When your answers are correct, all columns and rows will add to the same number.

A. LANGOSTAS   E. DEVIL   I. TERN   M. BIRDS
B. HATO   F. MALARIA   J. MOTHER   N. MELON
C. TAYLOR   G. KEG   K. SEVENTY   O. TREE
D. BELL   H. WATER   L. BAD   P. RAFT

1. They attacked Phillip.
2. Illness that struck Timothy
3. Timothy & Phillip each had 1/2 cup of it to celebrate landfall.
4. At first Phillip was too afraid to climb it.
5. The cat was ___ luck.
6. Author Theodore
7. Clawless lobsters Timothy caught for food
8. I wouldn't even be here with you if it wasn't for my ____.
9. Timothy was over ___ years old.
10. Sound that alerted Phillip his rescuers were coming
11. Ship Phillip & his mother took towards Miami
12. After the sinking of the ___, Phillip began to understand that war meant death and destruction.
13. Shape of the island
14. ____'s Mouth; name of the area of the cays
15. They lashed the water ___ to a tree trunk.
16. It carried Timothy, Phillip & the cat

A=	B=	C=	D=
E=	F=	G=	H=
I=	J=	K=	L=
M=	N=	O=	P=

The Cay Unit Magic Squares 3 Answer Key

Match the definition with the vocabulary word. Put your answers in the magic squares below. When your answers are correct, all columns and rows will add to the same number.

A. LANGOSTAS E. DEVIL   I. TERN   M. BIRDS
B. HATO   F. MALARIA J. MOTHER   N. MELON
C. TAYLOR   G. KEG   K. SEVENTY   O. TREE
D. BELL   H. WATER   L. BAD   P. RAFT

1. They attacked Phillip.
2. Illness that struck Timothy
3. Timothy & Phillip each had 1/2 cup of it to celebrate landfall.
4. At first Phillip was too afraid to climb it.
5. The cat was ___ luck.
6. Author Theodore
7. Clawless lobsters Timothy caught for food
8. I wouldn't even be here with you if it wasn't for my ____.
9. Timothy was over ___ years old.
10. Sound that alerted Phillip his rescuers were coming
11. Ship Phillip & his mother took towards Miami
12. After the sinking of the ___, Phillip began to understand that war meant death and destruction.
13. Shape of the island
14. ____'s Mouth; name of the area of the cays
15. They lashed the water ___ to a tree trunk.
16. It carried Timothy, Phillip & the cat

A=7	B=11	C=6	D=10
E=14	F=2	G=15	H=3
I=12	J=8	K=9	L=5
M=1	N=13	O=4	P=16

The Cay Unit Magic Squares 4

Match the definition with the vocabulary word. Put your answers in the magic squares below. When your answers are correct, all columns and rows will add to the same number.

A. HATO
B. HENRIK
C. NAZIS
D. JULY
E. ROPE
F. TAYLOR
G. GRAPE
H. FISH
I. MOTHER
J. BAD
K. CORAL
L. HUT
M. AMERICAN
N. HELP
O. TREE
P. TIMOTHY

1. At first Phillip was too afraid to climb it.
2. The cat was ___ luck.
3. Phillip learned to do this to feed himself.
4. Ship Phillip & his mother took towards Miami
5. Month the hurricane hit
6. Timothy made this with vines for Phillip.
7. It made navigating around the cays difficult.
8. Word they spelled on the beach in stones
9. Author Theodore
10. They sent U-boats to destroy ships.
11. Nationality of Phillip and Timothy
12. It was blown away.
13. I wouldn't even be here with you if it wasn't for my ____.
14. Negro man who cared for Phillip
15. Phillip's Dutch friend
16. Phillip used these oily leaves to make black smoke.

A=	B=	C=	D=
E=	F=	G=	H=
I=	J=	K=	L=
M=	N=	O=	P=

The Cay Unit Magic Squares 4 Answer Key

Match the definition with the vocabulary word. Put your answers in the magic squares below. When your answers are correct, all columns and rows will add to the same number.

A. HATO
B. HENRIK
C. NAZIS
D. JULY
E. ROPE
F. TAYLOR
G. GRAPE
H. FISH
I. MOTHER
J. BAD
K. CORAL
L. HUT
M. AMERICAN
N. HELP
O. TREE
P. TIMOTHY

1. At first Phillip was too afraid to climb it.
2. The cat was ___ luck.
3. Phillip learned to do this to feed himself.
4. Ship Phillip & his mother took towards Miami
5. Month the hurricane hit
6. Timothy made this with vines for Phillip.
7. It made navigating around the cays difficult.
8. Word they spelled on the beach in stones
9. Author Theodore
10. They sent U-boats to destroy ships.
11. Nationality of Phillip and Timothy
12. It was blown away.
13. I wouldn't even be here with you if it wasn't for my ____.
14. Negro man who cared for Phillip
15. Phillip's Dutch friend
16. Phillip used these oily leaves to make black smoke.

A=4	B=15	C=10	D=5
E=6	F=9	G=16	H=3
I=13	J=2	K=7	L=12
M=11	N=8	O=1	P=14

The Cay Unit Word Search 1

```
L B T W B K G T L N B T B H M E J P
W U E J A H A T O A P H E L P S U S
H T R L D R F A H I N N L A I U L L
S J N L L A C D L O R G R X N N Y F
R U Y R R A Y L B I M G O G K T D G
W M Z R R H I A K B A A H S T S S P
W B R U T H H M E R L M S W T R Z F
L I C O P S P E G I A A I W E A C J
G N M E S R S R E D R T F K G C S T
H I P M E M P I N G I S N M B I A S
T O Y H W C C C R E A A T R Z Z T N
R L T R A J O A I Y T T F A Y K S W
N O D D T D N N G T W F N T F S S R
M N O L E M F W H D L M N L C B H H
V Z D R R V L R T V M E A L E I A N
V I R G I N I A N D V R P E K R R F
W G M P R D C L V E O R R W T D K G
T A Y L O R T C S C F T S V N S S G
```

After the sinking of the ___, Phillip began to understand that war meant death and destruction. (4)
At first Phillip was too afraid to climb it. (4)
Author Theodore (6)
Clawless lobsters Timothy caught for food (9)
Evil spirit (5)
He regained his sight after operations. (7)
I wouldn't even be here with you if it wasn't for my ____. (6)
Illness that struck Timothy (7)
It carried Timothy, Phillip & the cat (4)
It made navigating around the cays difficult. (5)
It was blown away. (3)
Man vs. Nature, for example (8)
Month the hurricane hit (4)
Name of the cook's cat (4)
Nationality of Phillip and Timothy (8)
Negro man who cared for Phillip (7)
Phillip covered Timothy in grape leaves to protect him from the ____. (3)
Phillip fell off the raft into the water with _____. (6)
Phillip learned to do this to feed himself. (4)
Phillip lost his sight. He was ___. (5)
Phillip used these oily leaves to make black smoke. (5)
Phillip's Dutch friend (6)
Phillip's last name (7)
Place where Mr. Enright was sent to work (7)
Queen Emma was a ____ (6)
Shape of the island (5)
Ship Phillip & his mother took towards Miami (4)
Sound that alerted Phillip his rescuers were coming (4)
The Chinese crews on the ___ refused to sail. (7)
The Enrights were from this US state. (8)
The cat was ___ luck. (3)
They attacked Phillip. (5)
They lashed the water ___ to a tree trunk. (3)
They put a pebble in it each day. (3)
They sent U-boats to destroy ships. (5)
Timothy & Phillip each had 1/2 cup of it to celebrate landfall. (5)
Timothy asked Phillip to weave sleeping _____. (4)
Timothy called Phillip Young ___. (5)
Timothy made this with vines for Phillip. (4)
Timothy was over ___ years old. (7)
Timothy's home was on St. ____ (6)
Word they spelled on the beach in stones (4)
____'s Mouth; name of the area of the cays (5)

The Cay Unit Word Search 1 Answer Key

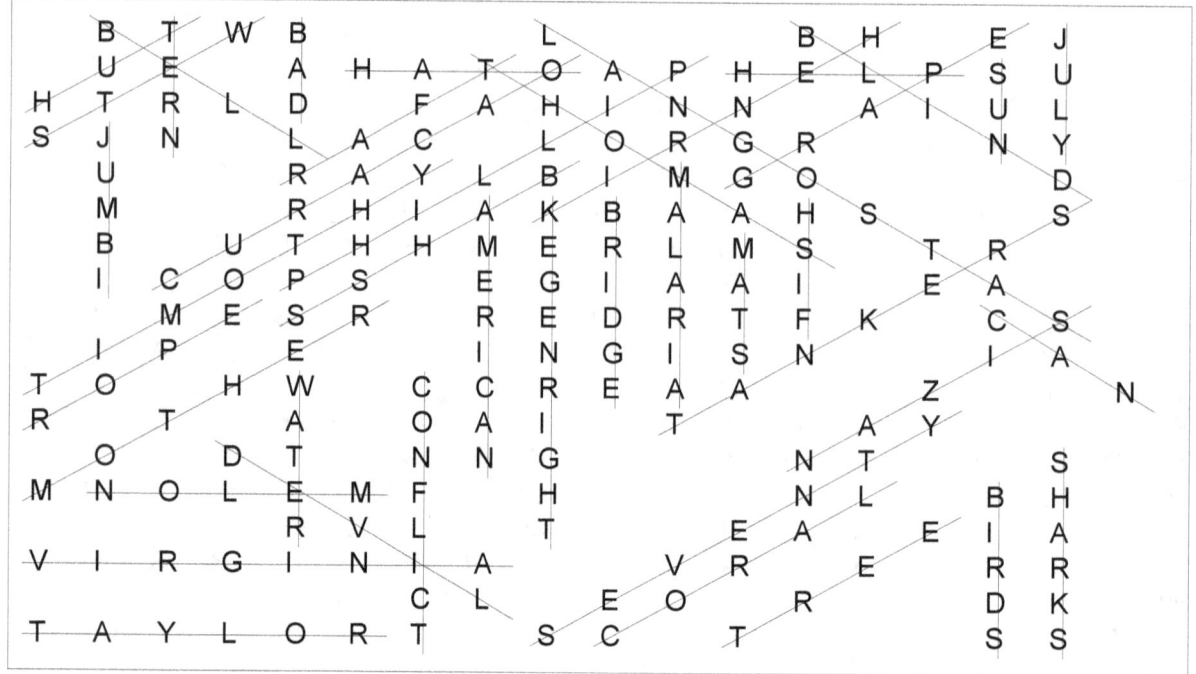

After the sinking of the ___, Phillip began to understand that war meant death and destruction. (4)
At first Phillip was too afraid to climb it. (4)
Author Theodore (6)
Clawless lobsters Timothy caught for food (9)
Evil spirit (5)
He regained his sight after operations. (7)
I wouldn't even be here with you if it wasn't for my ____. (6)
Illness that struck Timothy (7)
It carried Timothy, Phillip & the cat (4)
It made navigating around the cays difficult. (5)
It was blown away. (3)
Man vs. Nature, for example (8)
Month the hurricane hit (4)
Name of the cook's cat (4)
Nationality of Phillip and Timothy (8)
Negro man who cared for Phillip (7)
Phillip covered Timothy in grape leaves to protect him from the ____. (3)
Phillip fell off the raft into the water with ____. (6)
Phillip learned to do this to feed himself. (4)
Phillip lost his sight. He was ___. (5)
Phillip used these oily leaves to make black smoke. (5)

Phillip's Dutch friend (6)
Phillip's last name (7)
Place where Mr. Enright was sent to work (7)
Queen Emma was a ____ (6)
Shape of the island (5)
Ship Phillip & his mother took towards Miami (4)
Sound that alerted Phillip his rescuers were coming (4)
The Chinese crews on the ___ refused to sail. (7)
The Enrights were from this US state. (8)
The cat was ___ luck. (3)
They attacked Phillip. (5)
They lashed the water ___ to a tree trunk. (3)
They put a pebble in it each day. (3)
They sent U-boats to destroy ships. (5)
Timothy & Phillip each had 1/2 cup of it to celebrate landfall. (5)
Timothy asked Phillip to weave sleeping ____. (4)
Timothy called Phillip Young ___. (5)
Timothy made this with vines for Phillip. (4)
Timothy was over ___ years old. (7)
Timothy's home was on St. ____ (6)
Word they spelled on the beach in stones (4)
____'s Mouth; name of the area of the cays (5)

The Cay Unit Word Search 2

```
B A H S S A T S O G N A L B D H H F
M E J Z U L B N G K I A X N E U C N
E D L U N N A Y Z N R T I D N T F P
L E V L L Z D T I O H L K I R N E H
O O S L H Y C G C D B N B O I D M G
N D E L K I R K G L T M L V G E A F
P E V G L I Y G H R U Y B C H V T V
Y P E F V Z K T V J A P V R T I S X
P R N K T J R E V T L P E H I L H B
Z O T Y S H V S G E C T E X A D F J
C T Y R P C O H H R A L V Z M T G M
T Z H E B X F M M W K H Z P A I O E
Z P T N K K S O A N T J P C L M B Y
T V J I S L T H M S A C D C A O J T
R F G F Q H M W A L S Z Q F R T W Y
E W G E E T N E R R L C I I I H J W
E P O R N R E T A N K E R S A Y Y L
B I R D S N D S C A N S H H R A F T
```

After the sinking of the ___, Phillip began to understand that war meant death and destruction. (4)
At first Phillip was too afraid to climb it. (4)
Author Theodore (6)
Clawless lobsters Timothy caught for food (9)
Evil spirit (5)
I wouldn't even be here with you if it wasn't for my ____. (6)
Illness that struck Timothy (7)
It carried Timothy, Phillip & the cat (4)
It made navigating around the cays difficult. (5)
It was blown away. (3)
Man vs. Nature, for example (8)
Month the hurricane hit (4)
Name of the cook's cat (4)
Negro man who cared for Phillip (7)
Phillip covered Timothy in grape leaves to protect him from the ____. (3)
Phillip fell off the raft into the water with _____. (6)
Phillip learned to do this to feed himself. (4)
Phillip lost his sight. He was ___. (5)
Phillip used these oily leaves to make black smoke. (5)
Phillip's Dutch friend (6)
Phillip's last name (7)

Queen Emma was a ____ (6)
Shape of the island (5)
Ship Phillip & his mother took towards Miami (4)
Sound that alerted Phillip his rescuers were coming (4)
The Chinese crews on the ___ refused to sail. (7)
The Enrights were from this US state. (8)
The Hato was ___ on April 6, 1942. (9)
The cat was ___ luck. (3)
They attacked Phillip. (5)
They lashed the water ___ to a tree trunk. (3)
They put a pebble in it each day. (3)
They sent U-boats to destroy ships. (5)
Timothy & Phillip each had 1/2 cup of it to celebrate landfall. (5)
Timothy asked Phillip to weave sleeping _____. (4)
Timothy called Phillip Young ___. (5)
Timothy made this with vines for Phillip. (4)
Timothy was over ___ years old. (7)
Timothy's home was on St. ____ (6)
Where Mr. Enright worked (8)
Word they spelled on the beach in stones (4)
____'s Mouth; name of the area of the cays (5)

The Cay Unit Word Search 2 Answer Key

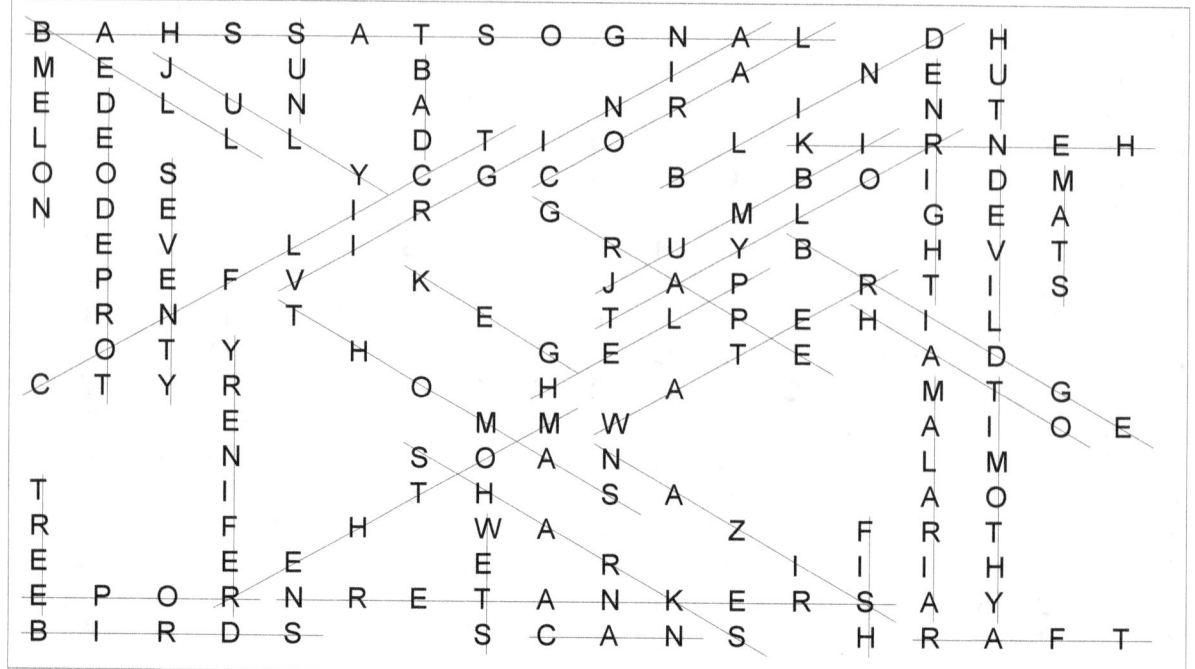

After the sinking of the ___, Phillip began to understand that war meant death and destruction. (4)
At first Phillip was too afraid to climb it. (4)
Author Theodore (6)
Clawless lobsters Timothy caught for food (9)
Evil spirit (5)
I wouldn't even be here with you if it wasn't for my ____. (6)
Illness that struck Timothy (7)
It carried Timothy, Phillip & the cat (4)
It made navigating around the cays difficult. (5)
It was blown away. (3)
Man vs. Nature, for example (8)
Month the hurricane hit (4)
Name of the cook's cat (4)
Negro man who cared for Phillip (7)
Phillip covered Timothy in grape leaves to protect him from the ____. (3)
Phillip fell off the raft into the water with _____. (6)
Phillip learned to do this to feed himself. (4)
Phillip lost his sight. He was ___. (5)
Phillip used these oily leaves to make black smoke. (5)
Phillip's Dutch friend (6)
Phillip's last name (7)

Queen Emma was a ____ (6)
Shape of the island (5)
Ship Phillip & his mother took towards Miami (4)
Sound that alerted Phillip his rescuers were coming (4)
The Chinese crews on the ___ refused to sail. (7)
The Enrights were from this US state. (8)
The Hato was ___ on April 6, 1942. (9)
The cat was ___ luck. (3)
They attacked Phillip. (5)
They lashed the water ___ to a tree trunk. (3)
They put a pebble in it each day. (3)
They sent U-boats to destroy ships. (5)
Timothy & Phillip each had 1/2 cup of it to celebrate landfall. (5)
Timothy asked Phillip to weave sleeping _____. (4)
Timothy called Phillip Young ___. (5)
Timothy made this with vines for Phillip. (4)
Timothy was over ___ years old. (7)
Timothy's home was on St. ____ (6)
Where Mr. Enright worked (8)
Word they spelled on the beach in stones (4)
____'s Mouth; name of the area of the cays (5)

The Cay Unit Word Search 3

```
K G H Y W K Z H T M M N M J Z T X S N Q
N P P B F R L M E A H H N U W L R T D X
A M E R I C A N R L J U X M O T H E R K
G L P F D T N F N A P U T B B M O W E M
L R O I S Z G K T R T Y L I M D J N N R
C F R S G N O K D I N A B Y E S D K W G
O B A H S S S O E A S Y Y P T C O R A L
N T C Y U X T P G G R H R L N H A G T J
F A N N L A A B B E B O A W O A O N E N
L N F T H R S R N F T A S R R R Z M R B
I K J Z G T Q I G N M D D X K Y T I A M
C E R M H P F D M P R H V L J S I V S S
T R H L N E R G P I D E V I L E M I C N
V S M O R R K E B H X J T Q M V O R U Z
F P L F C C N F P E I D N H J E T G R N
Z E B H M R B L I N D L P B S N H I A P
M Q D P I K G W B R R S L F X T Y N C C
N J L G F L B J K I Y Z N I Q Y C I A W
G G H Y W W N K C K N G M H P Z H A O D
N T T Q J H D X P N B Q Y Y L G G S Q X
```

AMERICAN	CORAL	HUT	NAZIS	TANKERS
BAD	CURACAO	JULY	PHILLIP	TAYLOR
BAHSS	DEVIL	JUMBI	RAFT	TERN
BELL	ENRIGHT	KEG	REFINERY	THOMAS
BIRDS	FISH	LANGOSTAS	ROPE	TIMOTHY
BLIND	GRAPE	MALARIA	SEVENTY	TORPEDOED
BRIDGE	HATO	MATS	SHARKS	TREE
CAN	HELP	MELON	STEW	VIRGINIA
CONFLICT	HENRIK	MOTHER	SUN	WATER

The Cay Unit Word Search 3 Answer Key

AMERICAN	CORAL	HUT	NAZIS	TANKERS
BAD	CURACAO	JULY	PHILLIP	TAYLOR
BAHSS	DEVIL	JUMBI	RAFT	TERN
BELL	ENRIGHT	KEG	REFINERY	THOMAS
BIRDS	FISH	LANGOSTAS	ROPE	TIMOTHY
BLIND	GRAPE	MALARIA	SEVENTY	TORPEDOED
BRIDGE	HATO	MATS	SHARKS	TREE
CAN	HELP	MELON	STEW	VIRGINIA
CONFLICT	HENRIK	MOTHER	SUN	WATER

The Cay Unit Word Search 4

```
V I R G I N I A Y T N E V E S G W C L T
R N G M W D Z K Y A Q D N W B N X W Y C
C B H L F E Z F V Z Y Y R W H A W F W I
Q V A Z G V X K M L R B W B E T H C B L
J Q T R K I B R T O V L S P A L E S A F
N C O R A L F T O R P E D O E D P R S N
Z P S C I E A L E J E D W V F I A A A O
E M H N Q G S N J R D E B M L F M C C S
N E D F T D A B G H N D A L T O I S U S
G L S D R I B Y E O C T I F H R T T R N
J O Z V R R M P L L S H S T E V Q E A J
M N K A T B A O D T P T H M P V K W C H
Z F L E H R K N T X S Q A C C N H J A R
B A B S G S M O T H E R R S A S U N O Y
M T H Q I T X U M X Y Z K T B M C V C T
S H E R F H G R W X C S S B F V C B M
R E F I N E R Y B L Y I F I J U L Y F V
Q J G N E R C F L B Z Z I N C Q Y L K L
F M G H S N I E S A W M S H B S T S F L
Y B S W T L B K N M Q S H M G M L S Q M
```

AMERICAN	CORAL	HUT	NAZIS	TANKERS
BAD	CURACAO	JULY	PHILLIP	TAYLOR
BAHSS	DEVIL	JUMBI	RAFT	TERN
BELL	ENRIGHT	KEG	REFINERY	THOMAS
BIRDS	FISH	LANGOSTAS	ROPE	TIMOTHY
BLIND	GRAPE	MALARIA	SEVENTY	TORPEDOED
BRIDGE	HATO	MATS	SHARKS	TREE
CAN	HELP	MELON	STEW	VIRGINIA
CONFLICT	HENRIK	MOTHER	SUN	WATER

The Cay Unit Word Search 4 Answer Key

```
V I R G I N I A Y T N E V E S         T
        D         A       W B         C
      H E         Y       H A A       I
      A V         L       B E  H  C   L
      T I B     T O R P E D O E D P   F
    C O R A L   O R       A I F R A   N
  E P  I E       R E      M L O I C   O
    M  N T A     N G      A T R   S   C
    E  D R B     G E      L H     T   S
    L  S R M     E O      I E     E
    O    T P     O T      S M     W
    N  K A A     T        P   N   J
       L T O     M O T H E R R A S U
     M H H R     U         K T M   N O
       E G               S
     R E F I N E R Y  L   F I   J U L Y
         R       Y  Z  A  S
               I E   N    H
               B K
```

AMERICAN	CORAL	HUT	NAZIS	TANKERS
BAD	CURACAO	JULY	PHILLIP	TAYLOR
BAHSS	DEVIL	JUMBI	RAFT	TERN
BELL	ENRIGHT	KEG	REFINERY	THOMAS
BIRDS	FISH	LANGOSTAS	ROPE	TIMOTHY
BLIND	GRAPE	MALARIA	SEVENTY	TORPEDOED
BRIDGE	HATO	MATS	SHARKS	TREE
CAN	HELP	MELON	STEW	VIRGINIA
CONFLICT	HENRIK	MOTHER	SUN	WATER

The Cay Unit Crossword 1

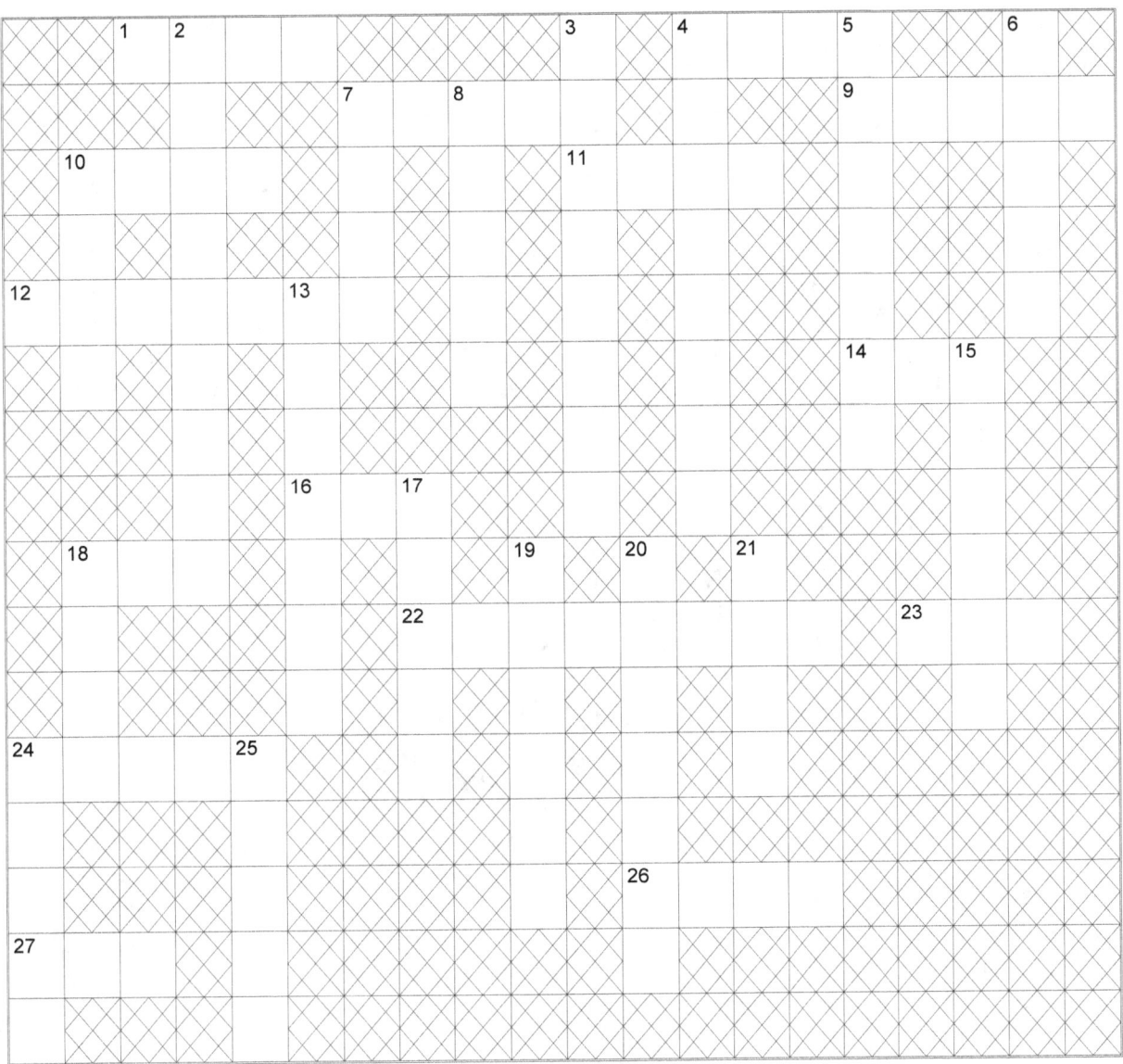

Across
1. Name of the cook's cat
4. Timothy made this with vines for Phillip.
7. Evil spirit
9. They sent U-boats to destroy ships.
10. After the sinking of the ___, Phillip began to understand that war meant death and destruction.
11. It carried Timothy, Phillip & the cat
12. Timothy was over ___ years old.
14. It was blown away.
16. They lashed the water ___ to a tree trunk.
18. The cat was ___ luck.
22. Nationality of Phillip and Timothy
23. They put a pebble in it each day.
24. Phillip lost his sight. He was ___.
26. Word they spelled on the beach in stones
27. Phillip covered Timothy in grape leaves to protect him from the ___.

Down
2. The Hato was ___ on April 6, 1942.
3. The Enrights were from this US state.
4. Where Mr. Enright worked
5. Phillip's last name
6. They attacked Phillip.
7. Month the hurricane hit
8. Shape of the island
10. At first Phillip was too afraid to climb it.
13. The Chinese crews on the ___ refused to sail.
15. Timothy's home was on St. ___
17. Phillip used these oily leaves to make black smoke.
18. Sound that alerted Phillip his rescuers were coming
19. Phillip's Dutch friend
20. Negro man who cared for Phillip
21. Ship Phillip & his mother took towards Miami
24. Timothy called Phillip Young ___.
25. ___'s Mouth; name of the area of the cays

The Cay Unit Crossword 1 Answer Key

	1 S	2 T	E	W		3 V		4 R	O	5 P	E		6 B
		O			7 J	U	8 M	B	I		9 N	A	Z	I	S
	10 T	E	R	N		U	E		11 R	A	F	T		R		R
		R		P		L	L		G		I		I		D
12 S	E	V	E	N	13 T	Y		O		I		N		G		S
		E		D		A			N		N		E	14 H	15 U	T
				O		N			I		R			T		H
				E		16 K	17 E	G		A		Y				O
	18 B	A	D			E	R		19 H		20 T		21 H		M
		E				R	22 A	M	E	R	I	C	A	N	23 C	A	N
		L					S		P		N		M		T		S
24 B	L	I	N	25 D					E		R		O		O
A				E					I				T	
H				V					K		26 H	E	L	P
27 S	U	N		I									Y	
S				L										

Across
1. Name of the cook's cat
4. Timothy made this with vines for Phillip.
7. Evil spirit
9. They sent U-boats to destroy ships.
10. After the sinking of the ___, Phillip began to understand that war meant death and destruction.
11. It carried Timothy, Phillip & the cat
12. Timothy was over ___ years old.
14. It was blown away.
16. They lashed the water ___ to a tree trunk.
18. The cat was ___ luck.
22. Nationality of Phillip and Timothy
23. They put a pebble in it each day.
24. Phillip lost his sight. He was ___.
26. Word they spelled on the beach in stones
27. Phillip covered Timothy in grape leaves to protect him from the ____.

Down
2. The Hato was ___ on April 6, 1942.
3. The Enrights were from this US state.
4. Where Mr. Enright worked
5. Phillip's last name
6. They attacked Phillip.
7. Month the hurricane hit
8. Shape of the island
10. At first Phillip was too afraid to climb it.
13. The Chinese crews on the ___ refused to sail.
15. Timothy's home was on St. ____
17. Phillip used these oily leaves to make black smoke.
18. Sound that alerted Phillip his rescuers were coming
19. Phillip's Dutch friend
20. Negro man who cared for Phillip
21. Ship Phillip & his mother took towards Miami
24. Timothy called Phillip Young ___.
25. ____'s Mouth; name of the area of the cays

The Cay Unit Crossword 2

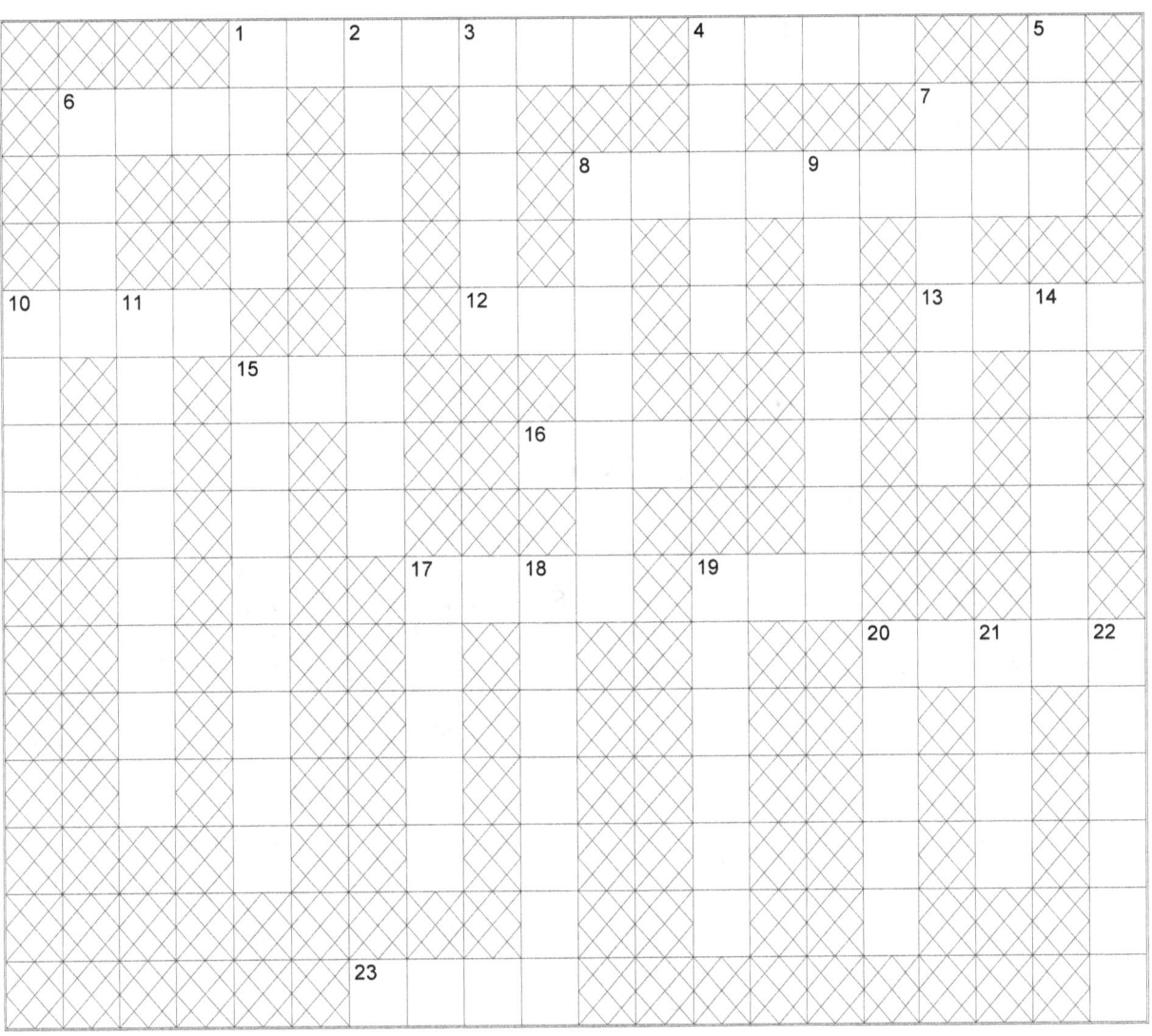

Across
1. Timothy was over ___ years old.
4. Sound that alerted Phillip his rescuers were coming
6. It carried Timothy, Phillip & the cat
8. The Hato was ___ on April 6, 1942.
10. After the sinking of the ___, Phillip began to understand that war meant death and destruction.
12. Phillip covered Timothy in grape leaves to protect him from the ____.
13. Ship Phillip & his mother took towards Miami
15. They put a pebble in it each day.
16. They lashed the water ___ to a tree trunk.
17. Timothy asked Phillip to weave sleeping _____.
19. It was blown away.
20. Timothy called Phillip Young ___.
23. Month the hurricane hit

Down
1. Name of the cook's cat
2. The Enrights were from this US state.
3. They sent U-boats to destroy ships.
4. They attacked Phillip.
5. The cat was ___ luck.
6. Timothy made this with vines for Phillip.
7. I wouldn't even be here with you if it wasn't for my ____.
8. The Chinese crews on the ___ refused to sail.
9. Phillip's last name
10. At first Phillip was too afraid to climb it.
11. Where Mr. Enright worked
14. Timothy's home was on St. ____
15. Man vs. Nature, for example
17. Shape of the island
18. Negro man who cared for Phillip
19. Phillip's Dutch friend
20. Phillip lost his sight. He was ___.
21. Word they spelled on the beach in stones
22. Phillip fell off the raft into the water with _____.

The Cay Unit Crossword 2 Answer Key

			1 S	2 E	3 V N	E	T	Y		4 B	E	L	L		5 B
		6 R	A	F	T	I		A		I			7 M		A
		O			E	R			8 T	O	R	9 P	E	D	O	E	D
		P			W		G	I	A		D		N		T
10 T	E	11 R	N			I		12 S	U	N		S	R		13 H	14 A	T	O
R		E		15 C	A	N				K			I		E	H
E		F		O		I		16 K	E	G			G		R	O
E		I		N		A		R					H			M
		N		F			17 M	18 A	T	S		19 H	U	T		A
		E		L			E		I			E			20 B	21 A	H	22 S
		R		I			L		M			N			L		E	H
		Y		C			O		O			R			I		L	A
				T			N		T			I			N		P	R
									H			K			D			K
					23 J	U	L	Y										S

Across
1. Timothy was over ___ years old.
4. Sound that alerted Phillip his rescuers were coming
6. It carried Timothy, Phillip & the cat
8. The Hato was ___ on April 6, 1942.
10. After the sinking of the ___, Phillip began to understand that war meant death and destruction.
12. Phillip covered Timothy in grape leaves to protect him from the ____.
13. Ship Phillip & his mother took towards Miami
15. They put a pebble in it each day.
16. They lashed the water ___ to a tree trunk.
17. Timothy asked Phillip to weave sleeping _____.
19. It was blown away.
20. Timothy called Phillip Young ___.
23. Month the hurricane hit

Down
1. Name of the cook's cat
2. The Enrights were from this US state.
3. They sent U-boats to destroy ships.
4. They attacked Phillip.
5. The cat was ___ luck.
6. Timothy made this with vines for Phillip.
7. I wouldn't even be here with you if it wasn't for my ____.
8. The Chinese crews on the ___ refused to sail.
9. Phillip's last name
10. At first Phillip was too afraid to climb it.
11. Where Mr. Enright worked
14. Timothy's home was on St. ____
15. Man vs. Nature, for example
17. Shape of the island
18. Negro man who cared for Phillip
19. Phillip's Dutch friend
20. Phillip lost his sight. He was ___.
21. Word they spelled on the beach in stones
22. Phillip fell off the raft into the water with _____.

The Cay Unit Crossword 3

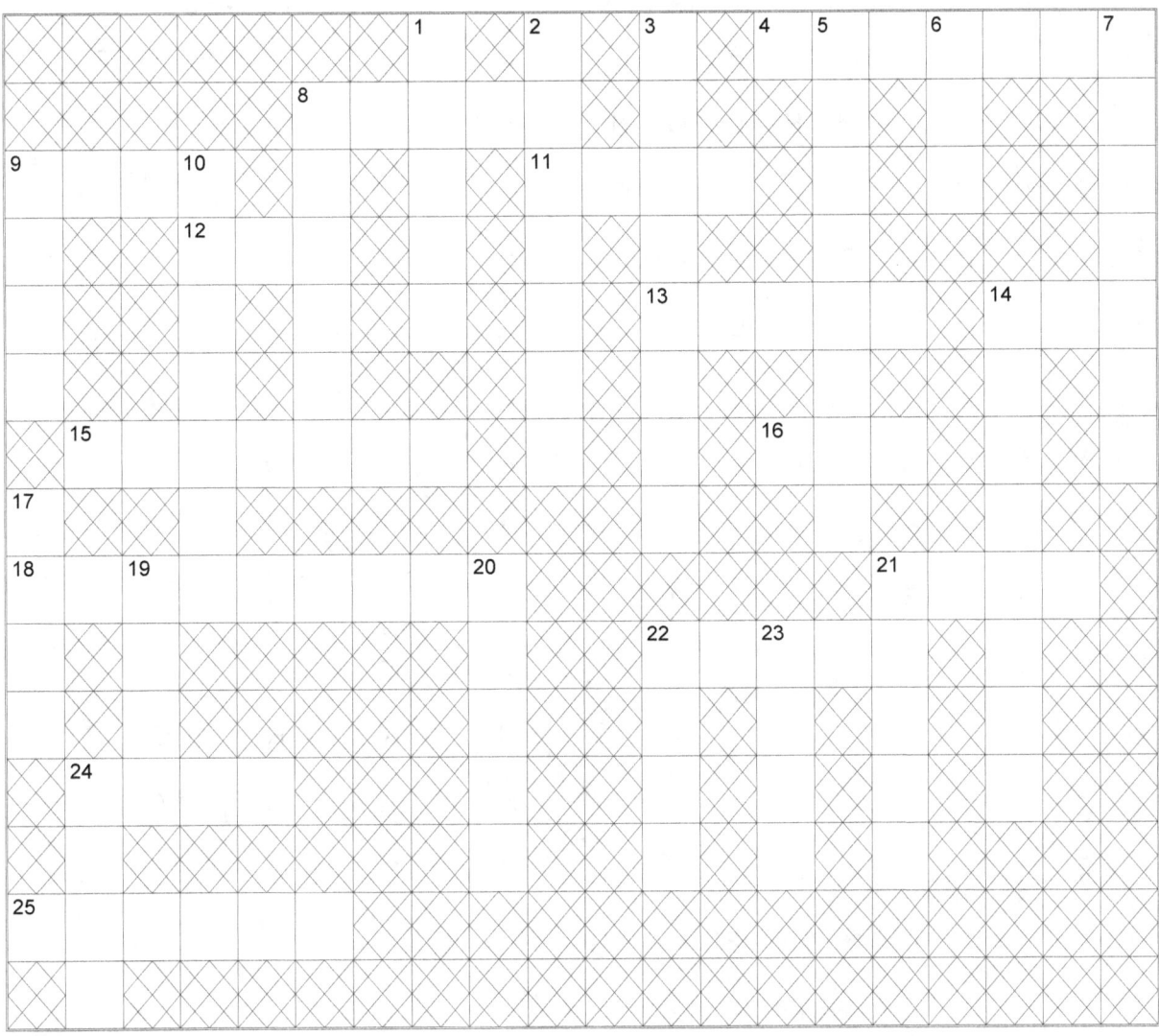

Across
4. The Chinese crews on the ___ refused to sail.
8. Shape of the island
9. Word they spelled on the beach in stones
11. It carried Timothy, Phillip & the cat
12. It was blown away.
13. They sent U-boats to destroy ships.
14. They put a pebble in it each day.
15. Illness that struck Timothy
16. The cat was ___ luck.
18. The Hato was ___ on April 6, 1942.
21. Sound that alerted Phillip his rescuers were coming
22. Evil spirit
24. After the sinking of the ___, Phillip began to understand that war meant death and destruction.
25. Phillip's Dutch friend

Down
1. Phillip lost his sight. He was ___.
2. Phillip's last name
3. Where Mr. Enright worked
5. Nationality of Phillip and Timothy
6. They lashed the water ___ to a tree trunk.
7. Timothy was over ___ years old.
8. I wouldn't even be here with you if it wasn't for my ___.
9. Ship Phillip & his mother took towards Miami
10. He regained his sight after operations.
14. Man vs. Nature, for example
17. Name of the cook's cat
19. Timothy made this with vines for Phillip.
20. ___'s Mouth; name of the area of the cays
21. They attacked Phillip.
22. Month the hurricane hit
23. Timothy asked Phillip to weave sleeping ___.
24. At first Phillip was too afraid to climb it.

The Cay Unit Crossword 3 Answer Key

					1 B		2 E		3 R		4 T	5 A		6 K	E	R	7 S
				8 M	E	L	O	N	E			M		E			E
9 H	E	L	10 P		O		I		11 R	A	F	T		E		G	V
A			12 H	U	T		N		I		I		R				E
T			I		H		D		13 N	A	Z	I	S		14 C	A	N
O			L		E				E		C				O		T
		15 M	A	L	A	R	I	A		T		R		16 B	A	D	N	Y
17 S			I								Y			N		F	
18 T	O	19 R	P	E	D	O	E	20 D					21 B	E	L	L
E		O						E			22 J	23 U	M	B	I		I
W		P						V			U	A		R		C
		24 T	E	R	N			I			L	T		D		T
		R						L			Y	S		S		
25 H	E	N	R	I	K											
		E														

Across
- 4. The Chinese crews on the ___ refused to sail.
- 8. Shape of the island
- 9. Word they spelled on the beach in stones
- 11. It carried Timothy, Phillip & the cat
- 12. It was blown away.
- 13. They sent U-boats to destroy ships.
- 14. They put a pebble in it each day.
- 15. Illness that struck Timothy
- 16. The cat was ___ luck.
- 18. The Hato was ___ on April 6, 1942.
- 21. Sound that alerted Phillip his rescuers were coming
- 22. Evil spirit
- 24. After the sinking of the ___, Phillip began to understand that war meant death and destruction.
- 25. Phillip's Dutch friend

Down
- 1. Phillip lost his sight. He was ___.
- 2. Phillip's last name
- 3. Where Mr. Enright worked
- 5. Nationality of Phillip and Timothy
- 6. They lashed the water ___ to a tree trunk.
- 7. Timothy was over ___ years old.
- 8. I wouldn't even be here with you if it wasn't for my ___.
- 9. Ship Phillip & his mother took towards Miami
- 10. He regained his sight after operations.
- 14. Man vs. Nature, for example
- 17. Name of the cook's cat
- 19. Timothy made this with vines for Phillip.
- 20. ___'s Mouth; name of the area of the cays
- 21. They attacked Phillip.
- 22. Month the hurricane hit
- 23. Timothy asked Phillip to weave sleeping ___.
- 24. At first Phillip was too afraid to climb it.

The Cay Unit Crosswod 4

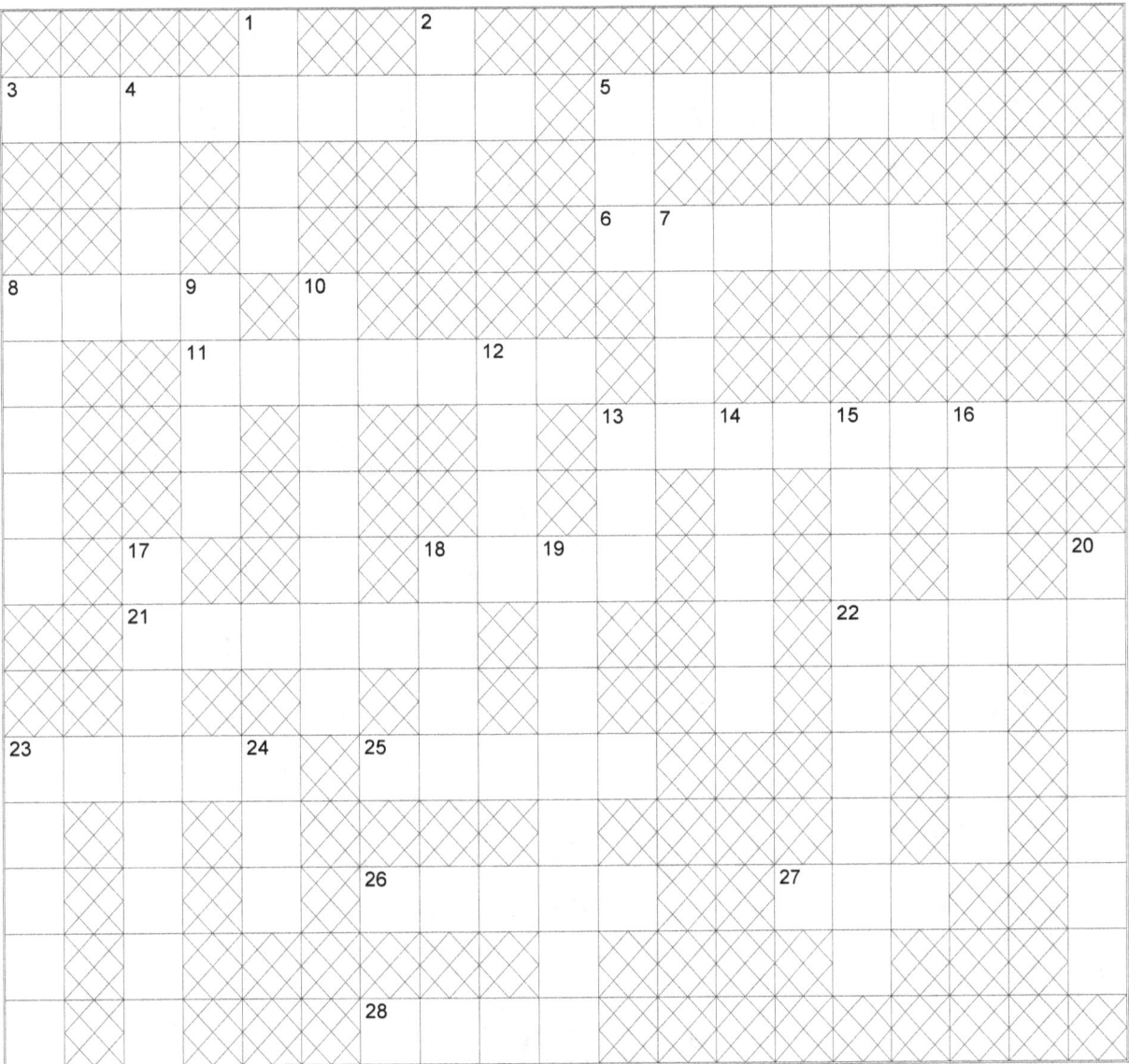

Across
3. The Hato was ___ on April 6, 1942.
5. Phillip's Dutch friend
6. Timothy's home was on St. ____
8. Timothy asked Phillip to weave sleeping _____.
11. The Chinese crews on the ___ refused to sail.
13. Man vs. Nature, for example
18. After the sinking of the ___, Phillip began to understand that war meant death and destruction.
21. I wouldn't even be here with you if it wasn't for my ____.
22. Phillip used these oily leaves to make black smoke.
23. They attacked Phillip.
25. ____'s Mouth; name of the area of the cays
26. Timothy & Phillip each had 1/2 cup of it to celebrate landfall.
27. The cat was ___ luck.
28. Month the hurricane hit

Down
1. Sound that alerted Phillip his rescuers were coming
2. They lashed the water ___ to a tree trunk.
4. It carried Timothy, Phillip & the cat
5. It was blown away.
7. Ship Phillip & his mother took towards Miami
8. Shape of the island
9. Name of the cook's cat
10. Phillip's last name
12. Timothy made this with vines for Phillip.
13. They put a pebble in it each day.
14. They sent U-boats to destroy ships.
15. Clawless lobsters Timothy caught for food
16. Place where Mr. Enright was sent to work
17. Nationality of Phillip and Timothy
18. At first Phillip was too afraid to climb it.
19. Where Mr. Enright worked
20. Timothy was over ___ years old.
23. Phillip lost his sight. He was ___.
24. Phillip covered Timothy in grape leaves to protect him from the ____.

The Cay Unit Crossword 4 Answer Key

Across
3. The Hato was ___ on April 6, 1942.
5. Phillip's Dutch friend
6. Timothy's home was on St. ____
8. Timothy asked Phillip to weave sleeping _____.
11. The Chinese crews on the ___ refused to sail.
13. Man vs. Nature, for example
18. After the sinking of the ___, Phillip began to understand that war meant death and destruction.
21. I wouldn't even be here with you if it wasn't for my ____.
22. Phillip used these oily leaves to make black smoke.
23. They attacked Phillip.
25. ____'s Mouth; name of the area of the cays
26. Timothy & Phillip each had 1/2 cup of it to celebrate landfall.
27. The cat was ___ luck.
28. Month the hurricane hit

Down
1. Sound that alerted Phillip his rescuers were coming
2. They lashed the water ___ to a tree trunk.
4. It carried Timothy, Phillip & the cat
5. It was blown away.
7. Ship Phillip & his mother took towards Miami
8. Shape of the island
9. Name of the cook's cat
10. Phillip's last name
12. Timothy made this with vines for Phillip.
13. They put a pebble in it each day.
14. They sent U-boats to destroy ships.
15. Clawless lobsters Timothy caught for food
16. Place where Mr. Enright was sent to work
17. Nationality of Phillip and Timothy
18. At first Phillip was too afraid to climb it.
19. Where Mr. Enright worked
20. Timothy was over ___ years old.
23. Phillip lost his sight. He was ___.
24. Phillip covered Timothy in grape leaves to protect him from the ____.

The Cay Unit

DEVIL	BAHSS	NAZIS	JULY	TANKERS
BRIDGE	LANGOSTAS	MATS	TORPEDOED	BLIND
CAN	SEVENTY	FREE SPACE	WATER	MALARIA
SHARKS	TAYLOR	SUN	CURACAO	KEG
VIRGINIA	MOTHER	BELL	CONFLICT	BAD

The Cay Unit

ENRIGHT	REFINERY	HUT	RAFT	THOMAS
TIMOTHY	HENRIK	CORAL	PHILLIP	GRAPE
AMERICAN	HATO	FREE SPACE	JUMBI	TERN
ROPE	BIRDS	MELON	STEW	HELP
BAD	CONFLICT	BELL	MOTHER	VIRGINIA

The Cay Unit

SEVENTY	HATO	REFINERY	TAYLOR	TERN
JULY	TORPEDOED	MATS	CURACAO	MOTHER
NAZIS	CONFLICT	FREE SPACE	SUN	BAD
CORAL	KEG	BIRDS	CAN	LANGOSTAS
HENRIK	MALARIA	TIMOTHY	BLIND	BELL

The Cay Unit

JUMBI	GRAPE	AMERICAN	MELON	HELP
THOMAS	SHARKS	STEW	FISH	DEVIL
ENRIGHT	TREE	FREE SPACE	HUT	BAHSS
ROPE	WATER	BRIDGE	TANKERS	PHILLIP
BELL	BLIND	TIMOTHY	MALARIA	HENRIK

The Cay Unit

CURACAO	HENRIK	ENRIGHT	HUT	CORAL
MATS	TREE	CONFLICT	WATER	JULY
VIRGINIA	SEVENTY	FREE SPACE	STEW	AMERICAN
MALARIA	BIRDS	TANKERS	BRIDGE	SHARKS
LANGOSTAS	REFINERY	TAYLOR	TERN	HATO

The Cay Unit

NAZIS	MOTHER	GRAPE	RAFT	TORPEDOED
BELL	CAN	ROPE	KEG	HELP
FISH	DEVIL	FREE SPACE	TIMOTHY	THOMAS
BAHSS	BLIND	PHILLIP	BAD	MELON
HATO	TERN	TAYLOR	REFINERY	LANGOSTAS

The Cay Unit

BIRDS	AMERICAN	STEW	WATER	HATO
SEVENTY	HENRIK	TREE	PHILLIP	RAFT
MELON	BAHSS	FREE SPACE	FISH	VIRGINIA
CURACAO	BELL	CONFLICT	TIMOTHY	TERN
CORAL	NAZIS	TORPEDOED	TANKERS	BRIDGE

The Cay Unit

BLIND	MOTHER	BAD	KEG	ENRIGHT
HELP	DEVIL	MATS	JULY	SUN
THOMAS	TAYLOR	FREE SPACE	CAN	HUT
MALARIA	ROPE	SHARKS	JUMBI	LANGOSTAS
BRIDGE	TANKERS	TORPEDOED	NAZIS	CORAL

The Cay Unit

PHILLIP	KEG	CAN	LANGOSTAS	TAYLOR
FISH	THOMAS	HUT	HELP	SUN
MALARIA	VIRGINIA	FREE SPACE	CORAL	ROPE
REFINERY	ENRIGHT	TIMOTHY	CURACAO	SHARKS
BRIDGE	JUMBI	HATO	MATS	BELL

The Cay Unit

NAZIS	STEW	TORPEDOED	MOTHER	SEVENTY
BIRDS	BAHSS	RAFT	TANKERS	GRAPE
JULY	HENRIK	FREE SPACE	MELON	AMERICAN
DEVIL	CONFLICT	BLIND	BAD	TERN
BELL	MATS	HATO	JUMBI	BRIDGE

The Cay Unit

MOTHER	STEW	RAFT	TIMOTHY	MATS
THOMAS	TREE	CURACAO	BIRDS	CORAL
CAN	JULY	FREE SPACE	BAD	FISH
PHILLIP	TERN	BELL	WATER	TORPEDOED
SEVENTY	BAHSS	NAZIS	BRIDGE	SHARKS

The Cay Unit

HELP	TANKERS	JUMBI	CONFLICT	KEG
HATO	GRAPE	HENRIK	DEVIL	BLIND
TAYLOR	HUT	FREE SPACE	MALARIA	ENRIGHT
SUN	AMERICAN	LANGOSTAS	MELON	REFINERY
SHARKS	BRIDGE	NAZIS	BAHSS	SEVENTY

The Cay Unit

DEVIL	SUN	REFINERY	VIRGINIA	MATS
KEG	MOTHER	MALARIA	PHILLIP	CURACAO
ENRIGHT	THOMAS	FREE SPACE	RAFT	CONFLICT
MELON	HATO	TERN	JULY	TORPEDOED
STEW	BAD	CORAL	BIRDS	BELL

The Cay Unit

TAYLOR	TREE	GRAPE	SHARKS	WATER
ROPE	TANKERS	AMERICAN	BRIDGE	FISH
BAHSS	CAN	FREE SPACE	HENRIK	LANGOSTAS
SEVENTY	HUT	NAZIS	JUMBI	BLIND
BELL	BIRDS	CORAL	BAD	STEW

The Cay Unit

NAZIS	SEVENTY	CORAL	TREE	JULY
SUN	KEG	VIRGINIA	MALARIA	MELON
MATS	BRIDGE	FREE SPACE	TERN	HUT
CONFLICT	CURACAO	BIRDS	ENRIGHT	FISH
TAYLOR	TANKERS	BAHSS	HENRIK	LANGOSTAS

The Cay Unit

WATER	BAD	TORPEDOED	RAFT	REFINERY
TIMOTHY	GRAPE	THOMAS	HELP	MOTHER
ROPE	AMERICAN	FREE SPACE	BELL	STEW
HATO	SHARKS	JUMBI	CAN	BLIND
LANGOSTAS	HENRIK	BAHSS	TANKERS	TAYLOR

The Cay Unit

HENRIK	BLIND	JUMBI	ROPE	FISH
KEG	SHARKS	RAFT	MATS	AMERICAN
SEVENTY	JULY	FREE SPACE	CORAL	MELON
MALARIA	PHILLIP	BIRDS	HELP	ENRIGHT
TAYLOR	BAHSS	CONFLICT	CURACAO	TIMOTHY

The Cay Unit

LANGOSTAS	REFINERY	BELL	VIRGINIA	BRIDGE
TREE	HUT	THOMAS	DEVIL	MOTHER
WATER	CAN	FREE SPACE	SUN	TANKERS
STEW	TERN	BAD	HATO	GRAPE
TIMOTHY	CURACAO	CONFLICT	BAHSS	TAYLOR

The Cay Unit

MOTHER	CURACAO	SHARKS	HENRIK	PHILLIP
CAN	BAHSS	JULY	ENRIGHT	HELP
CORAL	STEW	FREE SPACE	HUT	TAYLOR
THOMAS	MELON	SUN	BLIND	GRAPE
TERN	TIMOTHY	BELL	REFINERY	NAZIS

The Cay Unit

CONFLICT	BRIDGE	TORPEDOED	ROPE	RAFT
SEVENTY	DEVIL	WATER	BIRDS	LANGOSTAS
KEG	JUMBI	FREE SPACE	AMERICAN	MATS
TANKERS	VIRGINIA	TREE	MALARIA	HATO
NAZIS	REFINERY	BELL	TIMOTHY	TERN

The Cay Unit

PHILLIP	CAN	TIMOTHY	FISH	NAZIS
SUN	MATS	TANKERS	BRIDGE	BAD
ROPE	CONFLICT	FREE SPACE	HENRIK	JULY
AMERICAN	JUMBI	SHARKS	REFINERY	MELON
TERN	BIRDS	ENRIGHT	HELP	GRAPE

The Cay Unit

STEW	TAYLOR	BAHSS	LANGOSTAS	CURACAO
HATO	BLIND	HUT	RAFT	WATER
KEG	TORPEDOED	FREE SPACE	MALARIA	DEVIL
VIRGINIA	SEVENTY	THOMAS	TREE	MOTHER
GRAPE	HELP	ENRIGHT	BIRDS	TERN

The Cay Unit

BLIND	LANGOSTAS	TERN	MOTHER	KEG
BIRDS	MALARIA	MATS	TREE	BAD
HELP	TANKERS	FREE SPACE	TAYLOR	GRAPE
TIMOTHY	CAN	TORPEDOED	SEVENTY	MELON
CONFLICT	BAHSS	AMERICAN	STEW	RAFT

The Cay Unit

FISH	HENRIK	CURACAO	THOMAS	NAZIS
SHARKS	BELL	JULY	ENRIGHT	REFINERY
HATO	HUT	FREE SPACE	PHILLIP	ROPE
JUMBI	SUN	WATER	VIRGINIA	DEVIL
RAFT	STEW	AMERICAN	BAHSS	CONFLICT

The Cay Unit

HELP	PHILLIP	HUT	NAZIS	CURACAO
GRAPE	WATER	TERN	REFINERY	CAN
AMERICAN	DEVIL	FREE SPACE	ENRIGHT	BAHSS
MELON	CORAL	MALARIA	BAD	ROPE
HATO	STEW	BIRDS	BLIND	JUMBI

The Cay Unit

HENRIK	TREE	TANKERS	MOTHER	TIMOTHY
RAFT	BRIDGE	SUN	MATS	CONFLICT
SHARKS	TORPEDOED	FREE SPACE	VIRGINIA	JULY
FISH	TAYLOR	THOMAS	BELL	SEVENTY
JUMBI	BLIND	BIRDS	STEW	HATO

The Cay Unit

BELL	JUMBI	AMERICAN	HATO	SHARKS
TIMOTHY	RAFT	SEVENTY	HENRIK	CAN
CORAL	REFINERY	FREE SPACE	WATER	NAZIS
TANKERS	HUT	ROPE	BRIDGE	LANGOSTAS
KEG	CONFLICT	MALARIA	THOMAS	BIRDS

The Cay Unit

BLIND	GRAPE	BAHSS	DEVIL	PHILLIP
MOTHER	MATS	TORPEDOED	TREE	TAYLOR
ENRIGHT	JULY	FREE SPACE	BAD	VIRGINIA
CURACAO	MELON	FISH	TERN	SUN
BIRDS	THOMAS	MALARIA	CONFLICT	KEG

The Cay Unit

TORPEDOED	BELL	LANGOSTAS	BLIND	RAFT
MALARIA	ROPE	REFINERY	CORAL	CONFLICT
MOTHER	THOMAS	FREE SPACE	HELP	FISH
PHILLIP	CURACAO	HENRIK	ENRIGHT	MATS
MELON	JUMBI	AMERICAN	SHARKS	BAD

The Cay Unit

HATO	SEVENTY	JULY	TIMOTHY	TREE
BIRDS	TANKERS	DEVIL	TAYLOR	VIRGINIA
HUT	BAHSS	FREE SPACE	SUN	WATER
TERN	STEW	BRIDGE	NAZIS	CAN
BAD	SHARKS	AMERICAN	JUMBI	MELON

The Cay Unit

TORPEDOED	ENRIGHT	VIRGINIA	THOMAS	REFINERY
BAHSS	HENRIK	CONFLICT	DEVIL	TIMOTHY
WATER	NAZIS	FREE SPACE	TERN	BELL
TREE	TAYLOR	LANGOSTAS	JULY	BIRDS
MELON	SEVENTY	PHILLIP	HUT	SUN

The Cay Unit

BRIDGE	HATO	CORAL	SHARKS	BLIND
MOTHER	BAD	JUMBI	MATS	AMERICAN
ROPE	STEW	FREE SPACE	GRAPE	CAN
CURACAO	FISH	KEG	RAFT	MALARIA
SUN	HUT	PHILLIP	SEVENTY	MELON

The Cay Vocabulary Word List

No.	Word	Clue/Definition
1.	ALABASTER	Type of gypsum (white mineral) usually used for decorative plaster work
2.	ANGUISH	Extreme anxiety
3.	AWASH	Covered in water
4.	CATCHMENT	Device for collecting rain water
5.	CAY	Small, low island
6.	CEASE	Stop
7.	CELLOPHANE	Thin, transparent, waterproof material made from wood pulp
8.	COARSER	Rougher
9.	CREVICES	Narrow cracks
10.	DEBRIS	Fragments of broken things
11.	DIKES	Embankments to prevent flooding
12.	DISTILLED	Purified by boiling and condensing vapors
13.	DRONE	Low, humming sound
14.	EBONY	Brownish-black color
15.	EERIE	Unnerving or unusual in a way that suggests a connection with the supernatural
16.	FARE	Manage in doing something
17.	FLAILING	Thrashing or moving violently or uncontrollably
18.	FRET	Worry
19.	FRONDS	Large, divided leaves
20.	GROPED	Searched by feeling
21.	HONING	Sharpening
22.	IDLING	Operating but not in gear
23.	IRRITATING	Annoying; bothersome
24.	LEEWARD	Away from the wind
25.	LEGACY	Something handed down or left via will
26.	MALARIA	Recurring illness common in hot countries, characterized by chills & fever
27.	MURMURING	Speaking softly
28.	MUTINY	Organized rebellion against ship's captain or another authority
29.	NAVIGATION	Directing a vehicle's course
30.	PARCH	Dry out
31.	RECEDED	Went back or further away
32.	REFINERY	Place for processing raw materials such as oil or sugar
33.	SCOUR	Search carefully
34.	SPAN	Extend over or across something
35.	STOBS	Stakes
36.	TETHERED	Tied to
37.	TREACHEROUS	Involving hidden dangers
38.	UNRAVELED	Took apart the strands of rope or yarn
39.	VANISHED	Disappeared
40.	VEILS	Like curtains
41.	WELTED	Having ridges or bumps on the skin caused by being struck with something (like a whip)
42.	WRENCHING	Pulling or twisting away

The Cay Vocabulary Fill In The Blank 1

_____ 1. Recurring illness common in hot countries, characterized by chills & fever
_____ 2. Low, humming sound
_____ 3. Device for collecting rain water
_____ 4. Disappeared
_____ 5. Organized rebellion against ship's captain or another authority
_____ 6. Directing a vehicle's course
_____ 7. Speaking softly
_____ 8. Like curtains
_____ 9. Fragments of broken things
_____ 10. Large, divided leaves
_____ 11. Tied to
_____ 12. Worry
_____ 13. Involving hidden dangers
_____ 14. Type of gypsum (white mineral) usually used for decorative plaster work
_____ 15. Embankments to prevent flooding
_____ 16. Stakes
_____ 17. Annoying; bothersome
_____ 18. Dry out
_____ 19. Went back or further away
_____ 20. Search carefully

The Cay Vocabulary Fill In The Blank 1 Answer Key

MALARIA	1. Recurring illness common in hot countries, characterized by chills & fever
DRONE	2. Low, humming sound
CATCHMENT	3. Device for collecting rain water
VANISHED	4. Disappeared
MUTINY	5. Organized rebellion against ship's captain or another authority
NAVIGATION	6. Directing a vehicle's course
MURMURING	7. Speaking softly
VEILS	8. Like curtains
DEBRIS	9. Fragments of broken things
FRONDS	10. Large, divided leaves
TETHERED	11. Tied to
FRET	12. Worry
TREACHEROUS	13. Involving hidden dangers
ALABASTER	14. Type of gypsum (white mineral) usually used for decorative plaster work
DIKES	15. Embankments to prevent flooding
STOBS	16. Stakes
IRRITATING	17. Annoying; bothersome
PARCH	18. Dry out
RECEDED	19. Went back or further away
SCOUR	20. Search carefully

The Cay Vocabulary Fill In The Blank 2

_____ 1. Large, divided leaves

_____ 2. Disappeared

_____ 3. Like curtains

_____ 4. Directing a vehicle's course

_____ 5. Sharpening

_____ 6. Organized rebellion against ship's captain or another authority

_____ 7. Stakes

_____ 8. Place for processing raw materials such as oil or sugar

_____ 9. Thin, transparent, waterproof material made from wood pulp

_____ 10. Brownish-black color

_____ 11. Recurring illness common in hot countries, characterized by chills & fever

   12. Narrow cracks

_____ 13. Manage in doing something

_____ 14. Thrashing or moving violently or uncontrollably

_____ 15. Searched by feeling

_____ 16. Annoying; bothersome

_____ 17. Fragments of broken things

_____ 18. Speaking softly

_____ 19. Search carefully

_____ 20. Having ridges or bumps on the skin caused by being struck with something (like a whip)

The Cay Vocabulary Fill In The Blank 2 Answer Key

FRONDS	1. Large, divided leaves
VANISHED	2. Disappeared
VEILS	3. Like curtains
NAVIGATION	4. Directing a vehicle's course
HONING	5. Sharpening
MUTINY	6. Organized rebellion against ship's captain or another authority
STOBS	7. Stakes
REFINERY	8. Place for processing raw materials such as oil or sugar
CELLOPHANE	9. Thin, transparent, waterproof material made from wood pulp
EBONY	10. Brownish-black color
MALARIA	11. Recurring illness common in hot countries, characterized by chills & fever
CREVICES	12. Narrow cracks
FARE	13. Manage in doing something
FLAILING	14. Thrashing or moving violently or uncontrollably
GROPED	15. Searched by feeling
IRRITATING	16. Annoying; bothersome
DEBRIS	17. Fragments of broken things
MURMURING	18. Speaking softly
SCOUR	19. Search carefully
WELTED	20. Having ridges or bumps on the skin caused by being struck with something (like a whip)

The Cay Vocabulary Fill In The Blank 3

_____ 1. Having ridges or bumps on the skin caused by being struck with something (like a whip)

_____ 2. Low, humming sound

_____ 3. Unnerving or unusual in a way that suggests a connection with the supernatural

_____ 4. Thrashing or moving violently or uncontrollably

_____ 5. Like curtains

_____ 6. Recurring illness common in hot countries, characterized by chills & fever

_____ 7. Device for collecting rain water

_____ 8. Speaking softly

_____ 9. Pulling or twisting away

_____ 10. Involving hidden dangers

_____ 11. Took apart the strands of rope or yarn

_____ 12. Narrow cracks

_____ 13. Small, low island

_____ 14. Stakes

_____ 15. Searched by feeling

_____ 16. Place for processing raw materials such as oil or sugar

_____ 17. Something handed down or left via will

_____ 18. Tied to

_____ 19. Purified by boiling and condensing vapors

_____ 20. Search carefully

The Cay Vocabulary Fill In The Blank 3 Answer Key

WELTED	1. Having ridges or bumps on the skin caused by being struck with something (like a whip)
DRONE	2. Low, humming sound
EERIE	3. Unnerving or unusual in a way that suggests a connection with the supernatural
FLAILING	4. Thrashing or moving violently or uncontrollably
VEILS	5. Like curtains
MALARIA	6. Recurring illness common in hot countries, characterized by chills & fever
CATCHMENT	7. Device for collecting rain water
MURMURING	8. Speaking softly
WRENCHING	9. Pulling or twisting away
TREACHEROUS	10. Involving hidden dangers
UNRAVELED	11. Took apart the strands of rope or yarn
CREVICES	12. Narrow cracks
CAY	13. Small, low island
STOBS	14. Stakes
GROPED	15. Searched by feeling
REFINERY	16. Place for processing raw materials such as oil or sugar
LEGACY	17. Something handed down or left via will
TETHERED	18. Tied to
DISTILLED	19. Purified by boiling and condensing vapors
SCOUR	20. Search carefully

The Cay Vocabulary Fill In The Blank 4

_____ 1. Type of gypsum (white mineral) usually used for decorative plaster work
_____ 2. Narrow cracks
_____ 3. Large, divided leaves
_____ 4. Pulling or twisting away
_____ 5. Operating but not in gear
_____ 6. Purified by boiling and condensing vapors
_____ 7. Fragments of broken things
_____ 8. Stop
_____ 9. Brownish-black color
_____ 10. Took apart the strands of rope or yarn
_____ 11. Disappeared
_____ 12. Something handed down or left via will
_____ 13. Covered in water
_____ 14. Rougher
_____ 15. Extreme anxiety
_____ 16. Thin, transparent, waterproof material made from wood pulp
_____ 17. Dry out
_____ 18. Manage in doing something
_____ 19. Thrashing or moving violently or uncontrollably
_____ 20. Having ridges or bumps on the skin caused by being struck with something (like a whip)

The Cay Vocabulary Fill In The Blank 4 Answer Key

ALABASTER	1.	Type of gypsum (white mineral) usually used for decorative plaster work
CREVICES	2.	Narrow cracks
FRONDS	3.	Large, divided leaves
WRENCHING	4.	Pulling or twisting away
IDLING	5.	Operating but not in gear
DISTILLED	6.	Purified by boiling and condensing vapors
DEBRIS	7.	Fragments of broken things
CEASE	8.	Stop
EBONY	9.	Brownish-black color
UNRAVELED	10.	Took apart the strands of rope or yarn
VANISHED	11.	Disappeared
LEGACY	12.	Something handed down or left via will
AWASH	13.	Covered in water
COARSER	14.	Rougher
ANGUISH	15.	Extreme anxiety
CELLOPHANE	16.	Thin, transparent, waterproof material made from wood pulp
PARCH	17.	Dry out
FARE	18.	Manage in doing something
FLAILING	19.	Thrashing or moving violently or uncontrollably
WELTED	20.	Having ridges or bumps on the skin caused by being struck with something (like a whip)

The Cay Vocabulary Matching 1

___ 1. IDLING A. Low, humming sound
___ 2. FRET B. Thin, transparent, waterproof material made from wood pulp
___ 3. SPAN C. Manage in doing something
___ 4. DRONE D. Took apart the strands of rope or yarn
___ 5. VANISHED E. Worry
___ 6. DISTILLED F. Embankments to prevent flooding
___ 7. IRRITATING G. Covered in water
___ 8. DEBRIS H. Fragments of broken things
___ 9. CATCHMENT I. Having ridges or bumps on the skin caused by being struck with something (like a whip)
___10. AWASH J. Thrashing or moving violently or uncontrollably
___11. ANGUISH K. Purified by boiling and condensing vapors
___12. FARE L. Extend over or across something
___13. DIKES M. Annoying; bothersome
___14. MUTINY N. Rougher
___15. UNRAVELED O. Recurring illness common in hot countries, characterized by chills & fever
___16. WELTED P. Tied to
___17. CELLOPHANE Q. Something handed down or left via will
___18. MALARIA R. Organized rebellion against ship's captain or another authority
___19. CREVICES S. Extreme anxiety
___20. COARSER T. Sharpening
___21. HONING U. Went back or further away
___22. FLAILING V. Operating but not in gear
___23. RECEDED W. Device for collecting rain water
___24. TETHERED X. Disappeared
___25. LEGACY Y. Narrow cracks

The Cay Vocabulary Matching 1 Answer Key

V - 1. IDLING
E - 2. FRET
L - 3. SPAN
A - 4. DRONE
X - 5. VANISHED
K - 6. DISTILLED
M - 7. IRRITATING
H - 8. DEBRIS
W - 9. CATCHMENT
G - 10. AWASH
S - 11. ANGUISH
C - 12. FARE
F - 13. DIKES
R - 14. MUTINY
D - 15. UNRAVELED
I - 16. WELTED
B - 17. CELLOPHANE
O - 18. MALARIA
Y - 19. CREVICES
N - 20. COARSER
T - 21. HONING
J - 22. FLAILING
U - 23. RECEDED
P - 24. TETHERED
Q - 25. LEGACY

A. Low, humming sound
B. Thin, transparent, waterproof material made from wood pulp
C. Manage in doing something
D. Took apart the strands of rope or yarn
E. Worry
F. Embankments to prevent flooding
G. Covered in water
H. Fragments of broken things
I. Having ridges or bumps on the skin caused by being struck with something (like a whip)
J. Thrashing or moving violently or uncontrollably
K. Purified by boiling and condensing vapors
L. Extend over or across something
M. Annoying; bothersome
N. Rougher
O. Recurring illness common in hot countries, characterized by chills & fever
P. Tied to
Q. Something handed down or left via will
R. Organized rebellion against ship's captain or another authority
S. Extreme anxiety
T. Sharpening
U. Went back or further away
V. Operating but not in gear
W. Device for collecting rain water
X. Disappeared
Y. Narrow cracks

The Cay Vocabulary Matching 2

___ 1. MURMURING   A. Small, low island
___ 2. DISTILLED   B. Speaking softly
___ 3. ALABASTER   C. Annoying; bothersome
___ 4. VEILS   D. Extreme anxiety
___ 5. HONING   E. Device for collecting rain water
___ 6. LEEWARD   F. Directing a vehicle's course
___ 7. FLAILING   G. Sharpening
___ 8. ANGUISH   H. Stop
___ 9. IRRITATING   I. Type of gypsum (white mineral) usually used for decorative plaster work
___10. PARCH   J. Extend over or across something
___11. SCOUR   K. Rougher
___12. NAVIGATION   L. Worry
___13. MUTINY   M. Disappeared
___14. REFINERY   N. Search carefully
___15. CAY   O. Purified by boiling and condensing vapors
___16. DIKES   P. Place for processing raw materials such as oil or sugar
___17. VANISHED   Q. Organized rebellion against ship's captain or another authority
___18. SPAN   R. Like curtains
___19. CREVICES   S. Tied to
___20. COARSER   T. Embankments to prevent flooding
___21. DEBRIS   U. Narrow cracks
___22. CATCHMENT   V. Dry out
___23. TETHERED   W. Away from the wind
___24. CEASE   X. Fragments of broken things
___25. FRET   Y. Thrashing or moving violently or uncontrollably

The Cay Vocabulary Matching 2 Answer Key

B - 1. MURMURING
O - 2. DISTILLED
I - 3. ALABASTER
R - 4. VEILS
G - 5. HONING
W - 6. LEEWARD
Y - 7. FLAILING
D - 8. ANGUISH
C - 9. IRRITATING
V - 10. PARCH
N - 11. SCOUR
F - 12. NAVIGATION
Q - 13. MUTINY
P - 14. REFINERY
A - 15. CAY
T - 16. DIKES
M - 17. VANISHED
J - 18. SPAN
U - 19. CREVICES
K - 20. COARSER
X - 21. DEBRIS
E - 22. CATCHMENT
S - 23. TETHERED
H - 24. CEASE
L - 25. FRET

A. Small, low island
B. Speaking softly
C. Annoying; bothersome
D. Extreme anxiety
E. Device for collecting rain water
F. Directing a vehicle's course
G. Sharpening
H. Stop
I. Type of gypsum (white mineral) usually used for decorative plaster work
J. Extend over or across something
K. Rougher
L. Worry
M. Disappeared
N. Search carefully
O. Purified by boiling and condensing vapors
P. Place for processing raw materials such as oil or sugar
Q. Organized rebellion against ship's captain or another authority
R. Like curtains
S. Tied to
T. Embankments to prevent flooding
U. Narrow cracks
V. Dry out
W. Away from the wind
X. Fragments of broken things
Y. Thrashing or moving violently or uncontrollably

The Cay Vocabulary Matching 3

___ 1. LEEWARD   A. Small, low island
___ 2. HONING   B. Went back or further away
___ 3. DIKES   C. Away from the wind
___ 4. DRONE   D. Directing a vehicle's course
___ 5. VEILS   E. Involving hidden dangers
___ 6. TETHERED   F. Having ridges or bumps on the skin caused by being struck with something (like a whip)
___ 7. WELTED   G. Worry
___ 8. FLAILING   H. Low, humming sound
___ 9. CATCHMENT   I. Searched by feeling
___ 10. TREACHEROUS   J. Embankments to prevent flooding
___ 11. RECEDED   K. Something handed down or left via will
___ 12. CAY   L. Brownish-black color
___ 13. MURMURING   M. Device for collecting rain water
___ 14. IRRITATING   N. Annoying; bothersome
___ 15. FRONDS   O. Manage in doing something
___ 16. FARE   P. Like curtains
___ 17. CELLOPHANE   Q. Large, divided leaves
___ 18. GROPED   R. Took apart the strands of rope or yarn
___ 19. FRET   S. Speaking softly
___ 20. UNRAVELED   T. Thrashing or moving violently or uncontrollably
___ 21. EBONY   U. Sharpening
___ 22. ANGUISH   V. Thin, transparent, waterproof material made from wood pulp
___ 23. PARCH   W. Dry out
___ 24. NAVIGATION   X. Extreme anxiety
___ 25. LEGACY   Y. Tied to

The Cay Vocabulary Matching 3 Answer Key

C - 1. LEEWARD
U - 2. HONING
J - 3. DIKES
H - 4. DRONE
P - 5. VEILS
Y - 6. TETHERED
F - 7. WELTED
T - 8. FLAILING
M - 9. CATCHMENT
E - 10. TREACHEROUS
B - 11. RECEDED
A - 12. CAY
S - 13. MURMURING
N - 14. IRRITATING
Q - 15. FRONDS
O - 16. FARE
V - 17. CELLOPHANE
I - 18. GROPED
G - 19. FRET
R - 20. UNRAVELED
L - 21. EBONY
X - 22. ANGUISH
W - 23. PARCH
D - 24. NAVIGATION
K - 25. LEGACY

A. Small, low island
B. Went back or further away
C. Away from the wind
D. Directing a vehicle's course
E. Involving hidden dangers
F. Having ridges or bumps on the skin caused by being struck with something (like a whip)
G. Worry
H. Low, humming sound
I. Searched by feeling
J. Embankments to prevent flooding
K. Something handed down or left via will
L. Brownish-black color
M. Device for collecting rain water
N. Annoying; bothersome
O. Manage in doing something
P. Like curtains
Q. Large, divided leaves
R. Took apart the strands of rope or yarn
S. Speaking softly
T. Thrashing or moving violently or uncontrollably
U. Sharpening
V. Thin, transparent, waterproof material made from wood pulp
W. Dry out
X. Extreme anxiety
Y. Tied to

The Cay Vocabulary Matching 4

___ 1. CELLOPHANE   A. Large, divided leaves
___ 2. FRET   B. Unnerving or unusual in a way that suggests a connection with the supernatural
___ 3. EERIE   C. Sharpening
___ 4. IRRITATING   D. Disappeared
___ 5. CEASE   E. Narrow cracks
___ 6. REFINERY   F. Type of gypsum (white mineral) usually used for decorative plaster work
___ 7. MALARIA   G. Embankments to prevent flooding
___ 8. MURMURING   H. Having ridges or bumps on the skin caused by being struck with something (like a whip)
___ 9. PARCH   I. Speaking softly
___10. GROPED   J. Place for processing raw materials such as oil or sugar
___11. VANISHED   K. Dry out
___12. FRONDS   L. Something handed down or left via will
___13. EBONY   M. Thin, transparent, waterproof material made from wood pulp
___14. IDLING   N. Operating but not in gear
___15. DIKES   O. Annoying; bothersome
___16. LEGACY   P. Fragments of broken things
___17. DEBRIS   Q. Pulling or twisting away
___18. CREVICES   R. Device for collecting rain water
___19. NAVIGATION   S. Directing a vehicle's course
___20. ALABASTER   T. Worry
___21. HONING   U. Recurring illness common in hot countries, characterized by chills & fever
___22. WRENCHING   V. Brownish-black color
___23. WELTED   W. Covered in water
___24. AWASH   X. Stop
___25. CATCHMENT   Y. Searched by feeling

The Cay Vocabulary Matching 4 Answer Key

M - 1.	CELLOPHANE	A.	Large, divided leaves
T - 2.	FRET	B.	Unnerving or unusual in a way that suggests a connection with the supernatural
B - 3.	EERIE	C.	Sharpening
O - 4.	IRRITATING	D.	Disappeared
X - 5.	CEASE	E.	Narrow cracks
J - 6.	REFINERY	F.	Type of gypsum (white mineral) usually used for decorative plaster work
U - 7.	MALARIA	G.	Embankments to prevent flooding
I - 8.	MURMURING	H.	Having ridges or bumps on the skin caused by being struck with something (like a whip)
K - 9.	PARCH	I.	Speaking softly
Y - 10.	GROPED	J.	Place for processing raw materials such as oil or sugar
D - 11.	VANISHED	K.	Dry out
A - 12.	FRONDS	L.	Something handed down or left via will
V - 13.	EBONY	M.	Thin, transparent, waterproof material made from wood pulp
N - 14.	IDLING	N.	Operating but not in gear
G - 15.	DIKES	O.	Annoying; bothersome
L - 16.	LEGACY	P.	Fragments of broken things
P - 17.	DEBRIS	Q.	Pulling or twisting away
E - 18.	CREVICES	R.	Device for collecting rain water
S - 19.	NAVIGATION	S.	Directing a vehicle's course
F - 20.	ALABASTER	T.	Worry
C - 21.	HONING	U.	Recurring illness common in hot countries, characterized by chills & fever
Q - 22.	WRENCHING	V.	Brownish-black color
H - 23.	WELTED	W.	Covered in water
W - 24.	AWASH	X.	Stop
R - 25.	CATCHMENT	Y.	Searched by feeling

The Cay Vocabulary Magic Squares 1

Match the definition with the vocabulary word. Put your answers in the magic squares below. When your answers are correct, all columns and rows will add to the same number.

A. DEBRIS
B. LEEWARD
C. FRONDS
D. EERIE
E. PARCH
F. IDLING
G. STOBS
H. HONING
I. DIKES
J. MALARIA
K. CELLOPHANE
L. COARSER
M. CAY
N. TREACHEROUS
O. MURMURING
P. UNRAVELED

1. Operating but not in gear
2. Embankments to prevent flooding
3. Speaking softly
4. Unnerving or unusual in a way that suggests a connection with the supernatural
5. Small, low island
6. Away from the wind
7. Sharpening
8. Thin, transparent, waterproof material made from wood pulp
9. Large, divided leaves
10. Took apart the strands of rope or yarn
11. Recurring illness common in hot countries, characterized by chills & fever
12. Dry out
13. Rougher
14. Stakes
15. Fragments of broken things
16. Involving hidden dangers

A=	B=	C=	D=
E=	F=	G=	H=
I=	J=	K=	L=
M=	N=	O=	P=

The Cay Vocabulary Magic Squares 1 Answer Key

Match the definition with the vocabulary word. Put your answers in the magic squares below. When your answers are correct, all columns and rows will add to the same number.

A. DEBRIS
B. LEEWARD
C. FRONDS
D. EERIE
E. PARCH
F. IDLING
G. STOBS
H. HONING
I. DIKES
J. MALARIA
K. CELLOPHANE
L. COARSER
M. CAY
N. TREACHEROUS
O. MURMURING
P. UNRAVELED

1. Operating but not in gear
2. Embankments to prevent flooding
3. Speaking softly
4. Unnerving or unusual in a way that suggests a connection with the supernatural
5. Small, low island
6. Away from the wind
7. Sharpening
8. Thin, transparent, waterproof material made from wood pulp
9. Large, divided leaves
10. Took apart the strands of rope or yarn
11. Recurring illness common in hot countries, characterized by chills & fever
12. Dry out
13. Rougher
14. Stakes
15. Fragments of broken things
16. Involving hidden dangers

A=15	B=6	C=9	D=4
E=12	F=1	G=14	H=7
I=2	J=11	K=8	L=13
M=5	N=16	O=3	P=10

The Cay Vocabulary Magic Squares 2

Match the definition with the vocabulary word. Put your answers in the magic squares below. When your answers are correct, all columns and rows will add to the same number.

A. EERIE   E. RECEDED   I. SPAN   M. VEILS
B. MALARIA   F. TREACHEROUS   J. MURMURING   N. STOBS
C. CEASE   G. LEEWARD   K. PARCH   O. VANISHED
D. DRONE   H. FRONDS   L. WELTED   P. TETHERED

1. Like curtains
2. Involving hidden dangers
3. Large, divided leaves
4. Disappeared
5. Having ridges or bumps on the skin caused by being struck with something (like a whip)
6. Stop
7. Unnerving or unusual in a way that suggests a connection with the supernatural
8. Speaking softly
9. Dry out
10. Low, humming sound
11. Recurring illness common in hot countries, characterized by chills & fever
12. Extend over or across something
13. Stakes
14. Went back or further away
15. Away from the wind
16. Tied to

A=	B=	C=	D=
E=	F=	G=	H=
I=	J=	K=	L=
M=	N=	O=	P=

The Cay Vocabulary Magic Squares 2 Answer Key

Match the definition with the vocabulary word. Put your answers in the magic squares below. When your answers are correct, all columns and rows will add to the same number.

A. EERIE
B. MALARIA
C. CEASE
D. DRONE
E. RECEDED
F. TREACHEROUS
G. LEEWARD
H. FRONDS
I. SPAN
J. MURMURING
K. PARCH
L. WELTED
M. VEILS
N. STOBS
O. VANISHED
P. TETHERED

1. Like curtains
2. Involving hidden dangers
3. Large, divided leaves
4. Disappeared
5. Having ridges or bumps on the skin caused by being struck with something (like a whip)
6. Stop
7. Unnerving or unusual in a way that suggests a connection with the supernatural
8. Speaking softly
9. Dry out
10. Low, humming sound
11. Recurring illness common in hot countries, characterized by chills & fever
12. Extend over or across something
13. Stakes
14. Went back or further away
15. Away from the wind
16. Tied to

A=7	B=11	C=6	D=10
E=14	F=2	G=15	H=3
I=12	J=8	K=9	L=5
M=1	N=13	O=4	P=16

The Cay Vocabulary Magic Squares 3

Match the definition with the vocabulary word. Put your answers in the magic squares below. When your answers are correct, all columns and rows will add to the same number.

A. LEGACY
B. WELTED
C. COARSER
D. VANISHED
E. ALABASTER
F. PARCH
G. SCOUR
H. CEASE
I. EBONY
J. FRET
K. MURMURING
L. VEILS
M. ANGUISH
N. IRRITATING
O. CREVICES
P. DISTILLED

1. Narrow cracks
2. Disappeared
3. Worry
4. Type of gypsum (white mineral) usually used for decorative plaster work
5. Brownish-black color
6. Dry out
7. Purified by boiling and condensing vapors
8. Rougher
9. Stop
10. Speaking softly
11. Something handed down or left via will
12. Annoying; bothersome
13. Having ridges or bumps on the skin caused by being struck with something (like a whip)
14. Extreme anxiety
15. Search carefully
16. Like curtains

A=	B=	C=	D=
E=	F=	G=	H=
I=	J=	K=	L=
M=	N=	O=	P=

The Cay Vocabulary Magic Squares 3 Answer Key

Match the definition with the vocabulary word. Put your answers in the magic squares below. When your answers are correct, all columns and rows will add to the same number.

A. LEGACY	E. ALABASTER	I. EBONY	M. ANGUISH
B. WELTED	F. PARCH	J. FRET	N. IRRITATING
C. COARSER	G. SCOUR	K. MURMURING	O. CREVICES
D. VANISHED	H. CEASE	L. VEILS	P. DISTILLED

1. Narrow cracks
2. Disappeared
3. Worry
4. Type of gypsum (white mineral) usually used for decorative plaster work
5. Brownish-black color
6. Dry out
7. Purified by boiling and condensing vapors
8. Rougher
9. Stop
10. Speaking softly
11. Something handed down or left via will
12. Annoying; bothersome
13. Having ridges or bumps on the skin caused by being struck with something (like a whip)
14. Extreme anxiety
15. Search carefully
16. Like curtains

A=11	B=13	C=8	D=2
E=4	F=6	G=15	H=9
I=5	J=3	K=10	L=16
M=14	N=12	O=1	P=7

The Cay Vocabulary Magic Squares 4

Match the definition with the vocabulary word. Put your answers in the magic squares below. When your answers are correct, all columns and rows will add to the same number.

A. MURMURING   E. VANISHED   I. PARCH   M. EBONY
B. REFINERY   F. LEEWARD   J. DIKES   N. NAVIGATION
C. LEGACY   G. ALABASTER   K. TREACHEROUS O. SCOUR
D. CELLOPHANE   H. AWASH   L. MALARIA   P. CAY

1. Search carefully
2. Embankments to prevent flooding
3. Covered in water
4. Speaking softly
5. Thin, transparent, waterproof material made from wood pulp
6. Disappeared
7. Involving hidden dangers
8. Directing a vehicle's course
9. Away from the wind
10. Something handed down or left via will
11. Brownish-black color
12. Recurring illness common in hot countries, characterized by chills & fever
13. Dry out
14. Small, low island
15. Place for processing raw materials such as oil or sugar
16. Type of gypsum (white mineral) usually used for decorative plaster work

A=	B=	C=	D=
E=	F=	G=	H=
I=	J=	K=	L=
M=	N=	O=	P=

The Cay Vocabulary Magic Squares 4 Answer Key

Match the definition with the vocabulary word. Put your answers in the magic squares below. When your answers are correct, all columns and rows will add to the same number.

A. MURMURING   E. VANISHED   I. PARCH   M. EBONY
B. REFINERY   F. LEEWARD   J. DIKES   N. NAVIGATION
C. LEGACY   G. ALABASTER   K. TREACHEROUS   O. SCOUR
D. CELLOPHANE H. AWASH   L. MALARIA   P. CAY

1. Search carefully
2. Embankments to prevent flooding
3. Covered in water
4. Speaking softly
5. Thin, transparent, waterproof material made from wood pulp
6. Disappeared
7. Involving hidden dangers
8. Directing a vehicle's course
9. Away from the wind
10. Something handed down or left via will
11. Brownish-black color
12. Recurring illness common in hot countries, characterized by chills & fever
13. Dry out
14. Small, low island
15. Place for processing raw materials such as oil or sugar
16. Type of gypsum (white mineral) usually used for decorative plaster work

A=4	B=15	C=10	D=5
E=6	F=9	G=16	H=3
I=13	J=2	K=7	L=12
M=11	N=8	O=1	P=14

The Cay Vocabulary Word Search 1

```
T R E A C H E R O U S D I K E S D T H X
L D J S W S D H J D R Z H V R E N K Q M
T E L C F A M H N O D S Q L B E R N V F
X E E F N W B O N E I M U R M U R I N G
J N D W V A R E R R W G B H V F W G E A
B A G I A F J E B P C Q C N S J N B I W
Z H W S S R H E C W S T O B S I S R R D
P P L R K T D B S R A P Q V H W A V R Y
K O F F E S I B F C E D Y C E L N A I Y
Q L R T C Y S L F L M V N C A I D N T D
J L E B Y O P L L K X E I M Y Y L I A X
R E T S A B A L A E R U O C S T D S T K
V C H S M I N R T W D E A C E E X H I N
R G G O L Y W B S D K G C V L S Z E N S
R E F I N E R Y E E E Z S E H I W D G W
S L N I R I Y C B L R R V C D S M R C T
Y G T C S C N Z O K G A R L X E O R E F
B U S G A H D G N R R A I F C P D Y A V
M J K R V Y P Q Y N P N T B E H R R S R
D M W E L T E D U K G B Y D S T E V E S
```

Annoying; bothersome (10)
Away from the wind (7)
Brownish-black color (5)
Covered in water (5)
Device for collecting rain water (9)
Disappeared (8)
Dry out (5)
Embankments to prevent flooding (5)
Extend over or across something (4)
Fragments of broken things (6)
Having ridges or bumps on the skin caused by being struck with something (like a whip) (6)
Involving hidden dangers (11)
Large, divided leaves (6)
Like curtains (5)
Low, humming sound (5)
Manage in doing something (4)
Narrow cracks (8)
Operating but not in gear (6)
Organized rebellion against ship's captain or another authority (6)
Place for processing raw materials such as oil or sugar (8)
Pulling or twisting away (9)
Purified by boiling and condensing vapors (9)
Recurring illness common in hot countries, characterized by chills & fever (7)
Rougher (7)
Search carefully (5)
Searched by feeling (6)
Sharpening (6)
Small, low island (3)
Something handed down or left via will (6)
Speaking softly (9)
Stakes (5)
Stop (5)
Thin, transparent, waterproof material made from wood pulp (10)
Thrashing or moving violently or uncontrollably (8)
Tied to (8)
Took apart the strands of rope or yarn (9)
Type of gypsum (white mineral) usually used for decorative plaster work (9)
Unnerving or unusual in a way that suggests a connection with the supernatural (5)
Went back or further away (7)
Worry (4)

The Cay Vocabulary Word Search 1 Answer Key

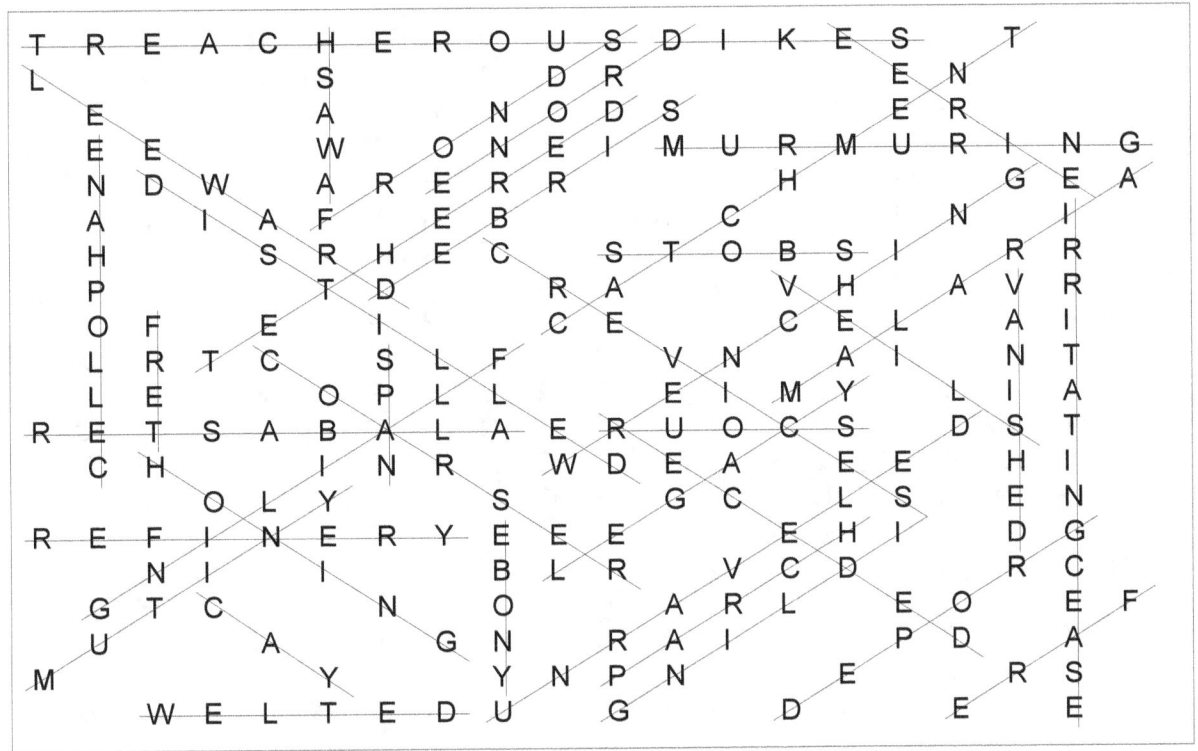

Annoying; bothersome (10)
Away from the wind (7)
Brownish-black color (5)
Covered in water (5)
Device for collecting rain water (9)
Disappeared (8)
Dry out (5)
Embankments to prevent flooding (5)
Extend over or across something (4)
Fragments of broken things (6)
Having ridges or bumps on the skin caused by being struck with something (like a whip) (6)
Involving hidden dangers (11)
Large, divided leaves (6)
Like curtains (5)
Low, humming sound (5)
Manage in doing something (4)
Narrow cracks (8)
Operating but not in gear (6)
Organized rebellion against ship's captain or another authority (6)
Place for processing raw materials such as oil or sugar (8)
Pulling or twisting away (9)
Purified by boiling and condensing vapors (9)
Recurring illness common in hot countries, characterized by chills & fever (7)
Rougher (7)
Search carefully (5)
Searched by feeling (6)
Sharpening (6)
Small, low island (3)
Something handed down or left via will (6)
Speaking softly (9)
Stakes (5)
Stop (5)
Thin, transparent, waterproof material made from wood pulp (10)
Thrashing or moving violently or uncontrollably (8)
Tied to (8)
Took apart the strands of rope or yarn (9)
Type of gypsum (white mineral) usually used for decorative plaster work (9)
Unnerving or unusual in a way that suggests a connection with the supernatural (5)
Went back or further away (7)
Worry (4)

The Cay Vocabulary Word Search 2

```
C R E V I C E S T D F W M A L A R I A G
Q F V A N I S H E D T E S X P Q R T Z S
V X L L A Z N D C E L L O P H A N E C F
F Q N A L N E Y L Z C T E T R L M T D N
M W A C I C G S L H A E T E T G B H Y N
N Y V D E L P U V X W D Y N W F J E K L
F J I R C A I C I W A H E R X A Z R G X
D M G X J Q S N V S S M L N D R R E J Z
K W A E E R I E G N H S Y H P E D D L T
S L T Y E K I N F C B A C C F E B N I J
Q C I N J L I Y T O C R G I P M F R H H
T W O W S H M A T Y A G N O D D R R I C
S R N U C M C S C P N E R E E I E H E S
D X X N R X H A L I R G L L T T K R C T
X N E S C S G N R Y G L E A S Y G E D Y
N R P D E A U Q N I V T A N N E S S C
W B H N L P M J I T A I B I I S B R P D
M Q O T S R L N S R N A T L N T O A J V
D R M F U B O I N G L U D B F Y N O L V
F G G M K H D U Q A M I D K Q K Y C K B
```

Annoying; bothersome (10)
Away from the wind (7)
Brownish-black color (5)
Covered in water (5)
Device for collecting rain water (9)
Directing a vehicle's course (10)
Disappeared (8)
Dry out (5)
Embankments to prevent flooding (5)
Extend over or across something (4)
Extreme anxiety (7)
Fragments of broken things (6)
Having ridges or bumps on the skin caused by being struck with something (like a whip) (6)
Large, divided leaves (6)
Like curtains (5)
Low, humming sound (5)
Manage in doing something (4)
Narrow cracks (8)
Operating but not in gear (6)
Organized rebellion against ship's captain or another authority (6)
Place for processing raw materials such as oil or sugar (8)
Pulling or twisting away (9)
Purified by boiling and condensing vapors (9)

Recurring illness common in hot countries, characterized by chills & fever (7)
Rougher (7)
Search carefully (5)
Searched by feeling (6)
Sharpening (6)
Small, low island (3)
Something handed down or left via will (6)
Speaking softly (9)
Stakes (5)
Stop (5)
Thin, transparent, waterproof material made from wood pulp (10)
Thrashing or moving violently or uncontrollably (8)
Tied to (8)
Took apart the strands of rope or yarn (9)
Type of gypsum (white mineral) usually used for decorative plaster work (9)
Unnerving or unusual in a way that suggests a connection with the supernatural (5)
Went back or further away (7)
Worry (4)

The Cay Vocabulary Word Search 2 Answer Key

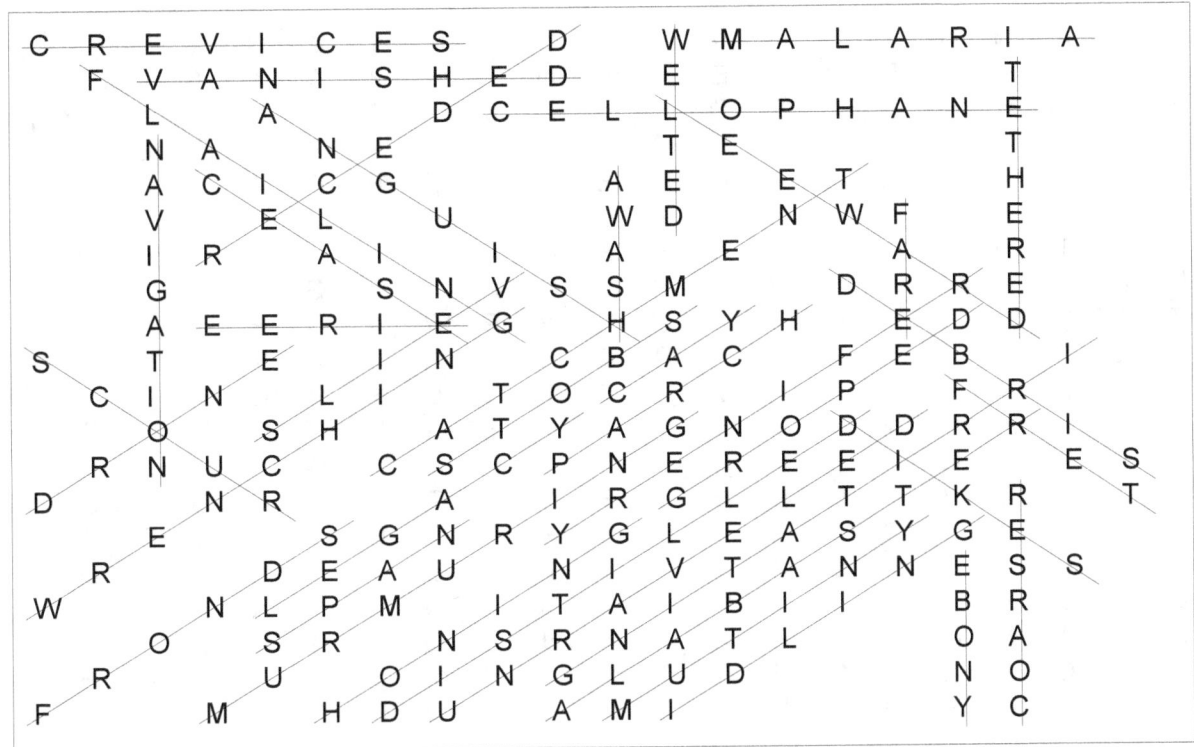

Annoying; bothersome (10)
Away from the wind (7)
Brownish-black color (5)
Covered in water (5)
Device for collecting rain water (9)
Directing a vehicle's course (10)
Disappeared (8)
Dry out (5)
Embankments to prevent flooding (5)
Extend over or across something (4)
Extreme anxiety (7)
Fragments of broken things (6)
Having ridges or bumps on the skin caused by being struck with something (like a whip) (6)
Large, divided leaves (6)
Like curtains (5)
Low, humming sound (5)
Manage in doing something (4)
Narrow cracks (8)
Operating but not in gear (6)
Organized rebellion against ship's captain or another authority (6)
Place for processing raw materials such as oil or sugar (8)
Pulling or twisting away (9)
Purified by boiling and condensing vapors (9)
Recurring illness common in hot countries, characterized by chills & fever (7)
Rougher (7)
Search carefully (5)
Searched by feeling (6)
Sharpening (6)
Small, low island (3)
Something handed down or left via will (6)
Speaking softly (9)
Stakes (5)
Stop (5)
Thin, transparent, waterproof material made from wood pulp (10)
Thrashing or moving violently or uncontrollably (8)
Tied to (8)
Took apart the strands of rope or yarn (9)
Type of gypsum (white mineral) usually used for decorative plaster work (9)
Unnerving or unusual in a way that suggests a connection with the supernatural (5)
Went back or further away (7)
Worry (4)

The Cay Vocabulary Word Search 3

```
S P A N S L I E V L E G A C Y A C A V W
M Q J B G F B X E Y N N R Y Z A K W A J
Z H O N K O A E D I V I H O T M X A N X
V T G L N M W R L D R R B C P P R S I H
S D N Y S A Q I E B E U H P R E T H S X
D I F A R T A L G W C M C N E D D I H S
D K T D V L L N X X E R R A F V U Q E N
K E L E F I I M N N D U A I I G B X D Y
W S W N T H G S T G E M P R N D R O N E
G M G S C H E A N P D R E A E X V T N G
P Q I N R C E I T C W T V L R P G V L Y
Q D E H I V N R E I S E Z A Y N C P S F
M R M V G O X L E A O V L M I S X G X Q
W L E D H W L M B D F N M T Z J Q Q N S
H R V B Y O J A U U N R A V E L E D S R
C Y S X P M L Z N T J T O L T D S I U D
H G J H K A W J B N I Q Z N K D R O F S
R J A X C K Z P W R N N Z Q D B C S T Y
T N C O A R S E R C K J Y T E S A E C H
E E R I E G N I L D I R H D F R E T H T
```

ALABASTER	DEBRIS	FRONDS	MUTINY	UNRAVELED
ANGUISH	DIKES	GROPED	NAVIGATION	VANISHED
AWASH	DISTILLED	HONING	PARCH	VEILS
CATCHMENT	DRONE	IDLING	RECEDED	WELTED
CAY	EBONY	IRRITATING	REFINERY	WRENCHING
CEASE	EERIE	LEEWARD	SCOUR	
CELLOPHANE	FARE	LEGACY	SPAN	
COARSER	FLAILING	MALARIA	STOBS	
CREVICES	FRET	MURMURING	TETHERED	

The Cay Vocabulary Word Search 3 Answer key

ALABASTER	DEBRIS	FRONDS	MUTINY	UNRAVELED
ANGUISH	DIKES	GROPED	NAVIGATION	VANISHED
AWASH	DISTILLED	HONING	PARCH	VEILS
CATCHMENT	DRONE	IDLING	RECEDED	WELTED
CAY	EBONY	IRRITATING	REFINERY	WRENCHING
CEASE	EERIE	LEEWARD	SCOUR	
CELLOPHANE	FARE	LEGACY	SPAN	
COARSER	FLAILING	MALARIA	STOBS	
CREVICES	FRET	MURMURING	TETHERED	

The Cay Vocabulary Word Search 4

```
I F N T R E A C H E R O U S S C O U R W
D L L B E F E S R L V G P B Z A X T M S
L S M A B T A R H E N J O Y D T Q D U F
I H U H I W H K I I V T P N Q C T C R Z
N W T S A L W E T E S I H O L H J E M C
G M I Q S H I A R K J D C B C M T L U J
B G N L Q D T N K E E C R E H E J L R C
G P Y V E I L S G H D X A C S N M O I S
K M F P R K K G S E O S P D C T G P N T
H C G R L E C I T D E N H Z N G M H G T
V O I V N S N L L U I G I M Q R T A A C
C A B J A A E R M Y N S L N J O G N L T
G R L R V W R Y A C P R T P G P D E A W
D S B M I Z Q F L Q V Z A I F E R N B X
R E Y S G R H Y A J B L S V L D A V A W
J R B S A L S T R L E V D M E L W S S J
J Q X R T Z L P I G B T N N Y L E R T B
Y R E N I F E R A F R Y O R E C E D E D
D Y N W O S S C W N A R R V C J L D R S
V V X C N W Y L J C D H F A N G U I S H
```

ALABASTER	DEBRIS	FRONDS	MUTINY	TREACHEROUS
ANGUISH	DIKES	GROPED	NAVIGATION	UNRAVELED
AWASH	DISTILLED	HONING	PARCH	VANISHED
CATCHMENT	DRONE	IDLING	RECEDED	VEILS
CAY	EBONY	IRRITATING	REFINERY	WELTED
CEASE	EERIE	LEEWARD	SCOUR	
CELLOPHANE	FARE	LEGACY	SPAN	
COARSER	FLAILING	MALARIA	STOBS	
CREVICES	FRET	MURMURING	TETHERED	

The Cay Vocabulary Word Search 4 Answer Key

ALABASTER	DEBRIS	FRONDS	MUTINY	TREACHEROUS
ANGUISH	DIKES	GROPED	NAVIGATION	UNRAVELED
AWASH	DISTILLED	HONING	PARCH	VANISHED
CATCHMENT	DRONE	IDLING	RECEDED	VEILS
CAY	EBONY	IRRITATING	REFINERY	WELTED
CEASE	EERIE	LEEWARD	SCOUR	
CELLOPHANE	FARE	LEGACY	SPAN	
COARSER	FLAILING	MALARIA	STOBS	
CREVICES	FRET	MURMURING	TETHERED	

The Cay Vocabulary Crossword 1

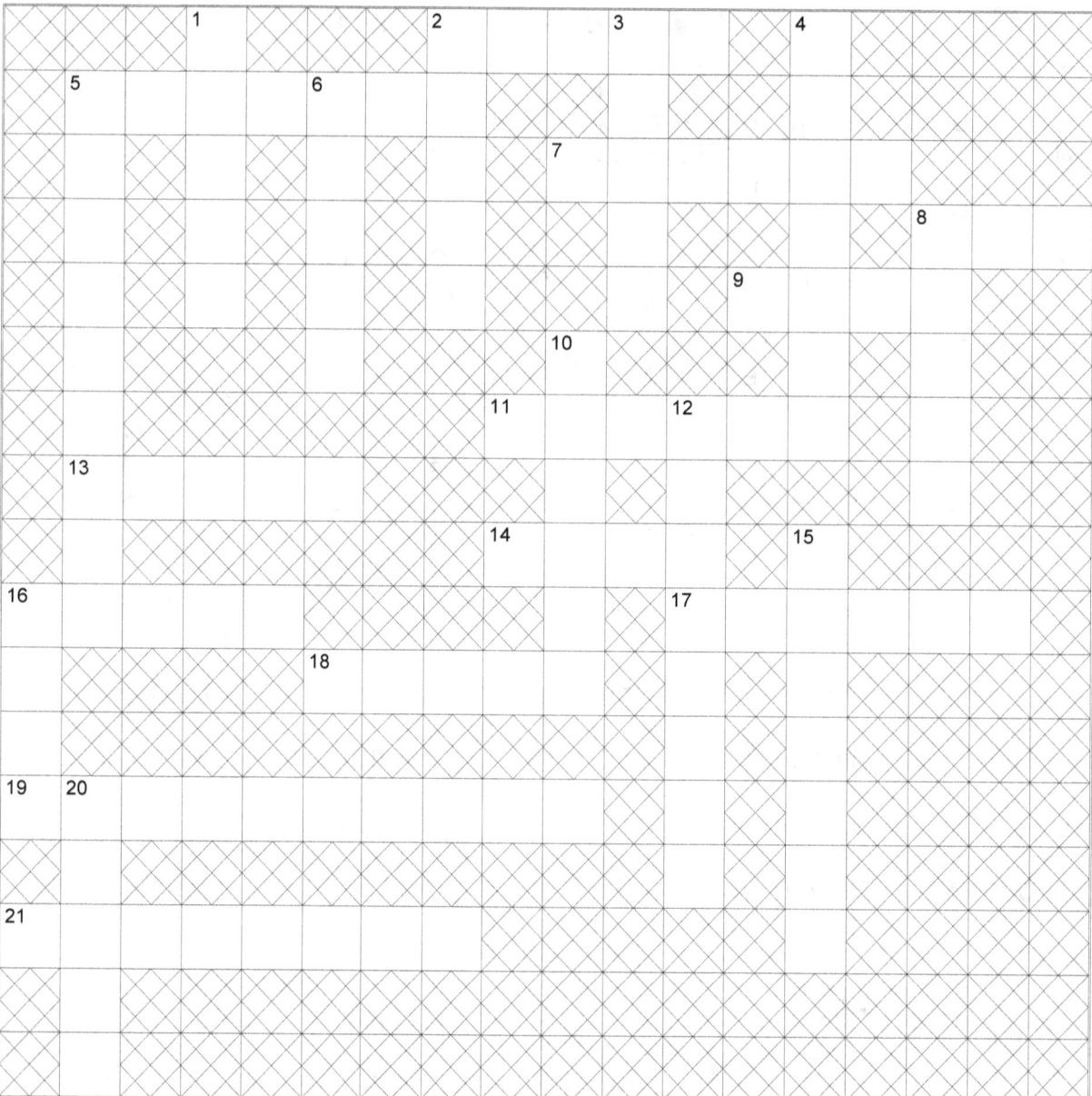

Across
2. Embankments to prevent flooding
5. Rougher
7. Searched by feeling
8. Small, low island
9. Manage in doing something
11. Having ridges or bumps on the skin caused by being struck with something (like a whip)
13. Brownish-black color
14. Worry
16. Stakes
17. Sharpening
18. Like curtains
19. Directing a vehicle's course
21. Disappeared

Down
1. Dry out
2. Low, humming sound
3. Unnerving or unusual in a way that suggests a connection with the supernatural
4. Away from the wind
5. Device for collecting rain water
6. Search carefully
8. Stop
10. Fragments of broken things
12. Tied to
15. Extreme anxiety
16. Extend over or across something
20. Covered in water

The Cay Vocabulary Crossword 1 Answer Key

		1 P		2 D	I	3 K	E	S	4 L		
	5 C	O	A	R	S	E	R		E		
	A	R		C	O	7 G	R	O	P	E	D
	T	C		O	N	I			W		8 C	A	Y
	C	H		U	E	E		9 F	A	R	E
	H			R		10 D		R		A
	M			11 W	E	L	12 T	E	D		S
13 E	B	O	N	Y		B	E			E
	N			14 F	R	E	T		15 A
16 S	T	O	B	S		I	17 H	O	N	I	N	G
P			18 V	E	I	L	S		G	
A						R		U
19 N	20 A	V	I	G	A	T	I	O	N	E		I
	W						D		S
21 V	A	N	I	S	H	E	D		H
	S
	H

Across
2. Embankments to prevent flooding
5. Rougher
7. Searched by feeling
8. Small, low island
9. Manage in doing something
11. Having ridges or bumps on the skin caused by being struck with something (like a whip)
13. Brownish-black color
14. Worry
16. Stakes
17. Sharpening
18. Like curtains
19. Directing a vehicle's course
21. Disappeared

Down
1. Dry out
2. Low, humming sound
3. Unnerving or unusual in a way that suggests a connection with the supernatural
4. Away from the wind
5. Device for collecting rain water
6. Search carefully
8. Stop
10. Fragments of broken things
12. Tied to
15. Extreme anxiety
16. Extend over or across something
20. Covered in water

The Cay Vocabulary Crossword 2

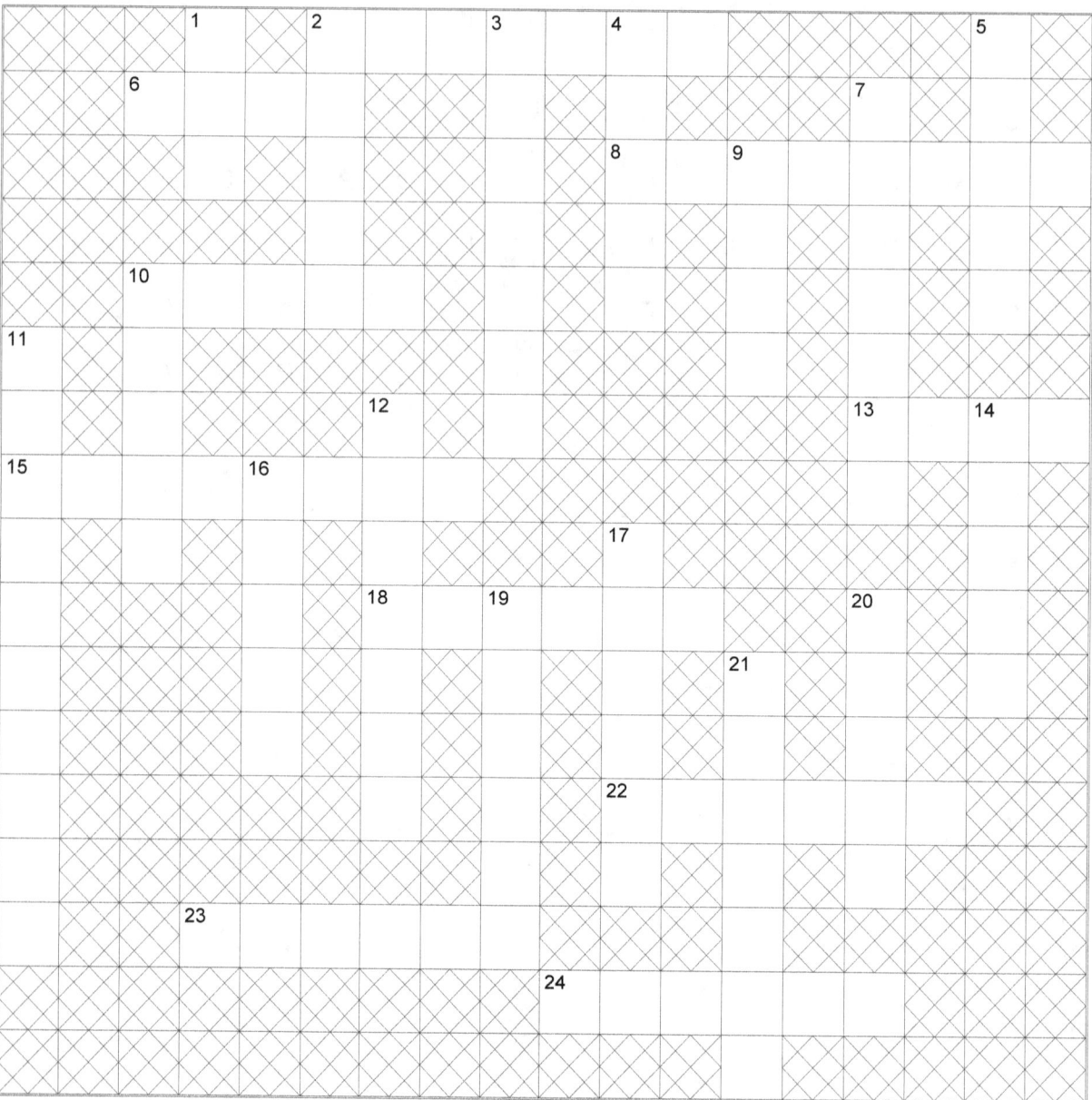

Across
2. Rougher
6. Manage in doing something
8. Place for processing raw materials such as oil or sugar
10. Embankments to prevent flooding
13. Extend over or across something
15. Disappeared
18. Having ridges or bumps on the skin caused by being struck with something (like a whip)
22. Operating but not in gear
23. Organized rebellion against ship's captain or another authority
24. Sharpening

Down
1. Small, low island
2. Stop
3. Went back or further away
4. Unnerving or unusual in a way that suggests a connection with the supernatural
5. Dry out
7. Extreme anxiety
9. Worry
10. Low, humming sound
11. Directing a vehicle's course
12. Away from the wind
14. Covered in water
16. Stakes
17. Fragments of broken things
19. Something handed down or left via will
20. Brownish-black color
21. Recurring illness common in hot countries, characterized by chills & fever

The Cay Vocabulary Crossword 2 Answer Key

			¹C		²C	O	A	³R	S	⁴E	R			⁵P	
		⁶F	A	R	E			E		E			⁷A	A	
			Y		A			C		⁸R	E	⁹F	I	N	E	R	Y
					S			E		I		R		G		C	
			¹⁰D	I	K	E	S	D		E		E		U		H	
¹¹N		R						E				T		I			
A		O			¹²L		D							¹³S	P	¹⁴A	N
¹⁵V	A	N	¹⁶I	S	H	E	D							H		W	
I		E		T		E				¹⁷D						A	
G				O		¹⁸W	E	¹⁹L	T	E	D			²⁰E		S	
A				B		A		E		B			²¹M		B		H
T				S		R		E		R			A		O		
I						D		G		²²I	D	L	I	N	G		
O								A		S			A		Y		
N			²³M	U	T	I	N	Y		R							
								²⁴H	O	N	I	N	G				
										A							

Across
2. Rougher
6. Manage in doing something
8. Place for processing raw materials such as oil or sugar
10. Embankments to prevent flooding
13. Extend over or across something
15. Disappeared
18. Having ridges or bumps on the skin caused by being struck with something (like a whip)
22. Operating but not in gear
23. Organized rebellion against ship's captain or another authority
24. Sharpening

Down
1. Small, low island
2. Stop
3. Went back or further away
4. Unnerving or unusual in a way that suggests a connection with the supernatural
5. Dry out
7. Extreme anxiety
9. Worry
10. Low, humming sound
11. Directing a vehicle's course
12. Away from the wind
14. Covered in water
16. Stakes
17. Fragments of broken things
19. Something handed down or left via will
20. Brownish-black color
21. Recurring illness common in hot countries, characterized by chills & fever

The Cay Vocabulary Crossword 3

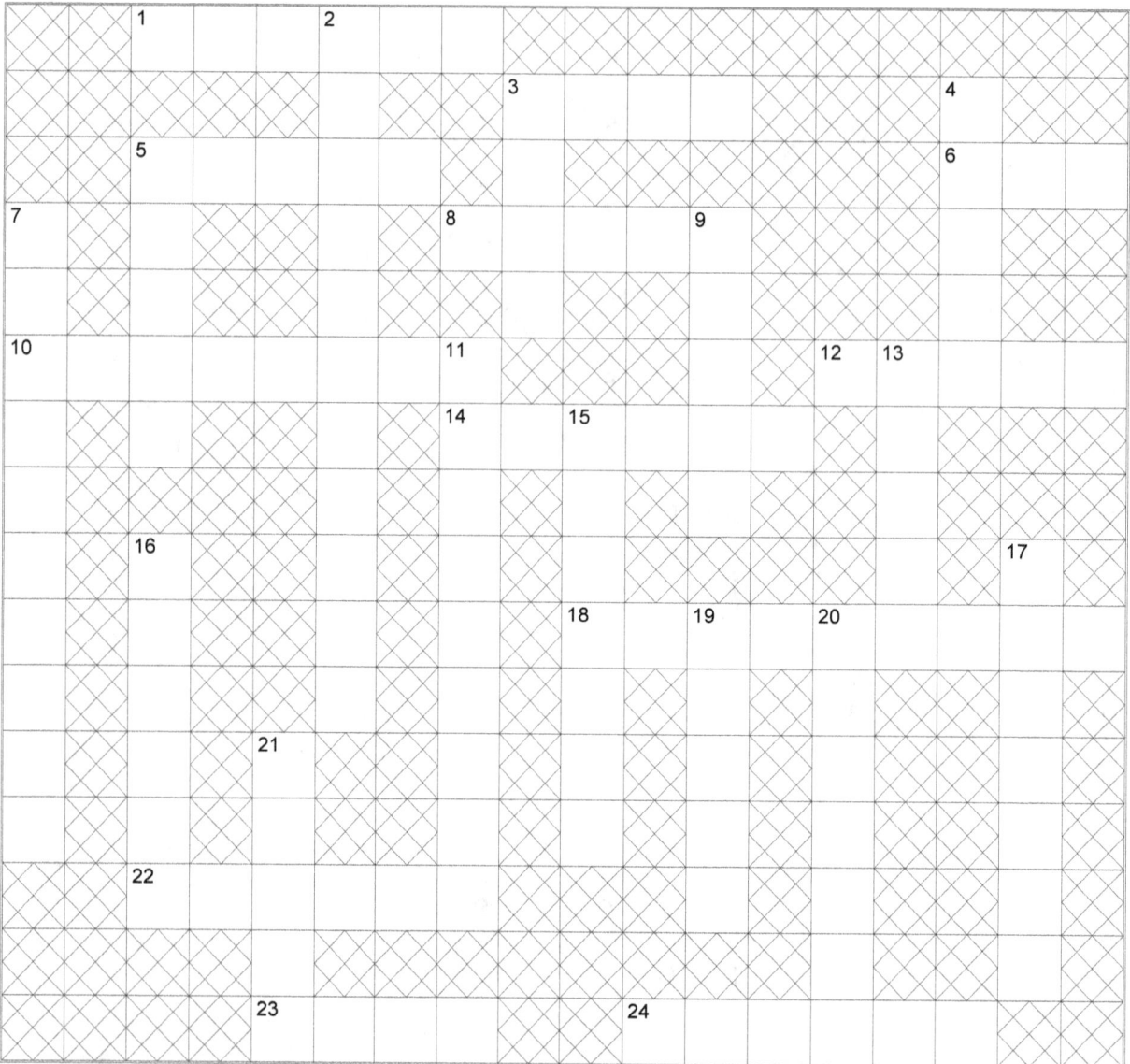

Across
1. Having ridges or bumps on the skin caused by being struck with something (like a whip)
3. Manage in doing something
5. Embankments to prevent flooding
6. Small, low island
8. Stop
10. Disappeared
12. Dry out
14. Operating but not in gear
18. Pulling or twisting away
22. Searched by feeling
23. Extend over or across something
24. Fragments of broken things

Down
2. Involving hidden dangers
3. Worry
4. Search carefully
5. Low, humming sound
7. Directing a vehicle's course
9. Brownish-black color
11. Purified by boiling and condensing vapors
13. Covered in water
15. Away from the wind
16. Sharpening
17. Extreme anxiety
19. Unnerving or unusual in a way that suggests a connection with the supernatural
20. Rougher
21. Stakes

The Cay Vocabulary Crossword 3 Answer Key

		¹W	E	L	²T	E	D						
					R			³F	A	R	E		⁴S
		⁵D	I	K	E	S		R				⁶C	A	Y
⁷N		R			A		⁸C	E	A	S	⁹E		O	
A		O			C		E				B		U	
¹⁰V	A	N	I	S	H	E	¹¹D				O		¹²P	¹³A	R	C	H
I		E			E		¹⁴I	D	¹⁵L	I	N	G		W	
G					R		S		E		Y			A	
A		¹⁶H			O		T		E					S		¹⁷A
									¹⁸W	¹⁹R	E	²⁰N	C	H	I	N	G
T		O			U		I		A		E		H			
I		N			S		L		R		E		O			G
O		I			²¹S		L		R		R		A			U
N		N			T		E		D		I		R			I
		²²G	R	O	P	E	D				E		S			S
					B								E			H
					²³S	P	A	N		²⁴D	E	B	R	I	S	

Across
1. Having ridges or bumps on the skin caused by being struck with something (like a whip)
3. Manage in doing something
5. Embankments to prevent flooding
6. Small, low island
8. Stop
10. Disappeared
12. Dry out
14. Operating but not in gear
18. Pulling or twisting away
22. Searched by feeling
23. Extend over or across something
24. Fragments of broken things

Down
2. Involving hidden dangers
3. Worry
4. Search carefully
5. Low, humming sound
7. Directing a vehicle's course
9. Brownish-black color
11. Purified by boiling and condensing vapors
13. Covered in water
15. Away from the wind
16. Sharpening
17. Extreme anxiety
19. Unnerving or unusual in a way that suggests a connection with the supernatural
20. Rougher
21. Stakes

The Cay Vocabulary Crossword 4

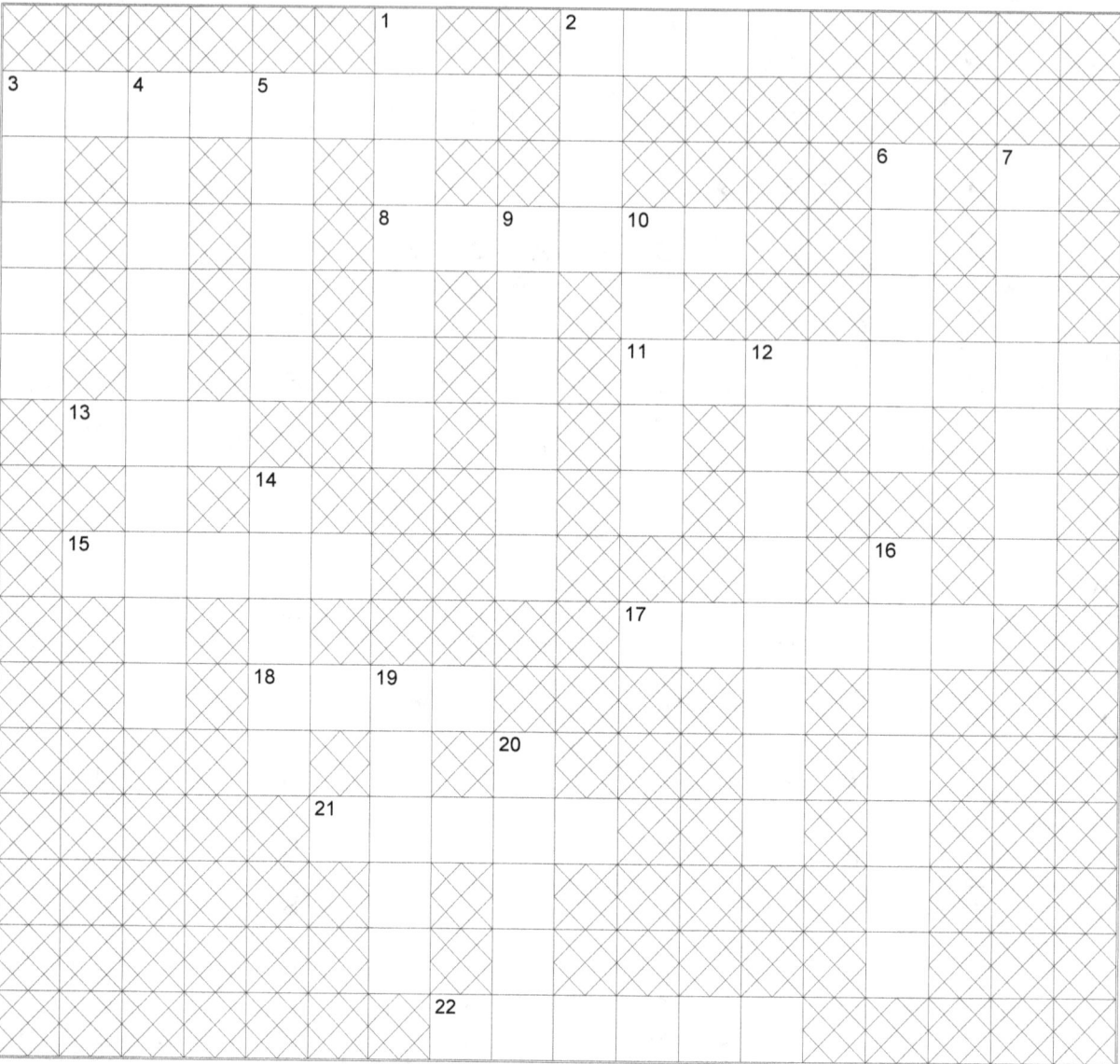

Across
2. Manage in doing something
3. Disappeared
8. Having ridges or bumps on the skin caused by being struck with something (like a whip)
11. Place for processing raw materials such as oil or sugar
13. Small, low island
15. Embankments to prevent flooding
17. Operating but not in gear
18. Extend over or across something
21. Dry out
22. Searched by feeling

Down
1. Away from the wind
2. Worry
3. Like curtains
4. Directing a vehicle's course
5. Stakes
6. Low, humming sound
7. Rougher
9. Something handed down or left via will
10. Unnerving or unusual in a way that suggests a connection with the supernatural
12. Thrashing or moving violently or uncontrollably
14. Stop
16. Extreme anxiety
19. Covered in water
20. Search carefully

The Cay Vocabulary Crossword 4 Answer Key

					¹L		²F	A	R	E		
³V	A	⁴N	I	⁵S	H	E	D				⁶	⁷
E		A		T		E		R			D	C
I		V		O	⁸W	E	⁹L	T	¹⁰E	D	R	O
L		I		B	A		E		E		O	A
S		G		S	R		G		¹¹R	¹²F	I	N	E	R	Y
	¹³C	A	Y		D		A		I	L		E	S
		T		¹⁴C			C		E	A			E
	¹⁵D	I	K	E	S		Y			I		¹⁶A	R
		O		A				¹⁷I	D	L	I	N	G
		N		¹⁸S	P	¹⁹A	N			I		G	
				E		W		²⁰S		N		U	
					²¹P	A	R	C	H		G		I
					S			O					S
					H			U					H
						²²G	R	O	P	E	D		

Across
2. Manage in doing something
3. Disappeared
8. Having ridges or bumps on the skin caused by being struck with something (like a whip)
11. Place for processing raw materials such as oil or sugar
13. Small, low island
15. Embankments to prevent flooding
17. Operating but not in gear
18. Extend over or across something
21. Dry out
22. Searched by feeling

Down
1. Away from the wind
2. Worry
3. Like curtains
4. Directing a vehicle's course
5. Stakes
6. Low, humming sound
7. Rougher
9. Something handed down or left via will
10. Unnerving or unusual in a way that suggests a connection with the supernatural
12. Thrashing or moving violently or uncontrollably
14. Stop
16. Extreme anxiety
19. Covered in water
20. Search carefully

The Cay Vocabulary Juggle Letters 1

1. REARSOC = 1. _____
   Rougher

2. EERECDD = 2. _____
   Went back or further away

3. RCSECVIE = 3. _____
   Narrow cracks

4. REIWNCGNH = 4. _____
   Pulling or twisting away

5. ANPS = 5. _____
   Extend over or across something

6. GDINLI = 6. _____
   Operating but not in gear

7. NGOHNI = 7. _____
   Sharpening

8. CCMTNTEAH = 8. _____
   Device for collecting rain water

9. IMYUNT = 9. _____
   Organized rebellion against ship's captain or another authority

10. PDEGOR =10. _____
    Searched by feeling

11. SANHIGU =11. _____
    Extreme anxiety

12. SRNOFD =12. _____
    Large, divided leaves

13. SEDBRI =13. _____
    Fragments of broken things

14. OTBSS =14. _____
    Stakes

15. RHPCA =15. _____
    Dry out

The Cay Vocabulary Juggle Letters 1 Answer Key

1. REARSOC = 1. COARSER
Rougher

2. EERECDD = 2. RECEDED
Went back or further away

3. RCSECVIE = 3. CREVICES
Narrow cracks

4. REIWNCGNH = 4. WRENCHING
Pulling or twisting away

5. ANPS = 5. SPAN
Extend over or across something

6. GDINLI = 6. IDLING
Operating but not in gear

7. NGOHNI = 7. HONING
Sharpening

8. CCMTNTEAH = 8. CATCHMENT
Device for collecting rain water

9. IMYUNT = 9. MUTINY
Organized rebellion against ship's captain or another authority

10. PDEGOR =10. GROPED
Searched by feeling

11. SANHIGU =11. ANGUISH
Extreme anxiety

12. SRNOFD =12. FRONDS
Large, divided leaves

13. SEDBRI =13. DEBRIS
Fragments of broken things

14. OTBSS =14. STOBS
Stakes

15. RHPCA =15. PARCH
Dry out

The Cay Vocabulary Juggle Letters 2

1. CRPAH = 1. _____
   Dry out

2. NPAS = 2. _____
   Extend over or across something

3. ASEEC = 3. _____
   Stop

4. HEORSCRETUA = 4. _____
   Involving hidden dangers

5. ITESLDILD = 5. _____
   Purified by boiling and condensing vapors

6. BSIEDR = 6. _____
   Fragments of broken things

7. CAY = 7. _____
   Small, low island

8. LEVRUENAD = 8. _____
   Took apart the strands of rope or yarn

9. TTREEHED = 9. _____
   Tied to

10. VNOIAGIATN = 10. _____
    Directing a vehicle's course

11. EERIE = 11. _____
    Unnerving or unusual in a way that suggests a connection with the supernatural

12. DCEDREE = 12. _____
    Went back or further away

13. TWEELD = 13. _____
    Having ridges or bumps on the skin caused by being struck with something (like a whip)

14. LDIIGN = 14. _____
    Operating but not in gear

15. ODRGPE = 15. _____
    Searched by feeling

The Cay Vocabulary Juggle Letters 2 Answer Key

1. CRPAH = 1. PARCH
Dry out

2. NPAS = 2. SPAN
Extend over or across something

3. ASEEC = 3. CEASE
Stop

4. HEORSCRETUA = 4. TREACHEROUS
Involving hidden dangers

5. ITESLDILD = 5. DISTILLED
Purified by boiling and condensing vapors

6. BSIEDR = 6. DEBRIS
Fragments of broken things

7. CAY = 7. CAY
Small, low island

8. LEVRUENAD = 8. UNRAVELED
Took apart the strands of rope or yarn

9. TTREEHED = 9. TETHERED
Tied to

10. VNOIAGIATN = 10. NAVIGATION
Directing a vehicle's course

11. EERIE = 11. EERIE
Unnerving or unusual in a way that suggests a connection with the supernatural

12. DCEDREE = 12. RECEDED
Went back or further away

13. TWEELD = 13. WELTED
Having ridges or bumps on the skin caused by being struck with something (like a whip)

14. LDIIGN = 14. IDLING
Operating but not in gear

15. ODRGPE = 15. GROPED
Searched by feeling

The Cay Vocabulary Juggle Letters 3

1. GINHNO   = 1. _____
                   Sharpening

2. OTSBS   = 2. _____
                   Stakes

3. UHGISAN   = 3. _____
                   Extreme anxiety

4. INGLID   = 4. _____
                   Operating but not in gear

5. IGMMNUURR   = 5. _____
                   Speaking softly

6. DREDCEE   = 6. _____
                   Went back or further away

7. AHCTEOSURRE = 7. _____
                   Involving hidden dangers

8. BALTAASER   = 8. _____
                   Type of gypsum (white mineral) usually used for decorative plaster work

9. EDRAEWL   = 9. _____
                   Away from the wind

10. RPDGOE   =10. _____
                   Searched by feeling

11. UTNMIY   =11. _____
                   Organized rebellion against ship's captain or another authority

12. RAAMALI   =12. _____
                   Recurring illness common in hot countries, characterized by chills & fever

13. SERBDI   =13. _____
                   Fragments of broken things

14. RIATIGIRTN =14. _____
                   Annoying; bothersome

15. TERF   =15. _____
                   Worry

The Cay Vocabulary Juggle Letters 3 Answer Key

1. GINHNO = 1. HONING
   Sharpening

2. OTSBS = 2. STOBS
   Stakes

3. UHGISAN = 3. ANGUISH
   Extreme anxiety

4. INGLID = 4. IDLING
   Operating but not in gear

5. IGMMNUURR = 5. MURMURING
   Speaking softly

6. DREDCEE = 6. RECEDED
   Went back or further away

7. AHCTEOSURRE = 7. TREACHEROUS
   Involving hidden dangers

8. BALTAASER = 8. ALABASTER
   Type of gypsum (white mineral) usually used for decorative plaster work

9. EDRAEWL = 9. LEEWARD
   Away from the wind

10. RPDGOE = 10. GROPED
    Searched by feeling

11. UTNMIY = 11. MUTINY
    Organized rebellion against ship's captain or another authority

12. RAAMALI = 12. MALARIA
    Recurring illness common in hot countries, characterized by chills & fever

13. SERBDI = 13. DEBRIS
    Fragments of broken things

14. RIATIGIRTN = 14. IRRITATING
    Annoying; bothersome

15. TERF = 15. FRET
    Worry

The Cay Vocabulary Juggle Letters 4

1. EARF = 1. _____
   Manage in doing something

2. RUGRNMMIU = 2. _____
   Speaking softly

3. SEDKI = 3. _____
   Embankments to prevent flooding

4. NFREERIY = 4. _____
   Place for processing raw materials such as oil or sugar

5. ILDTSELID = 5. _____
   Purified by boiling and condensing vapors

6. RTDEEHET = 6. _____
   Tied to

7. RPAHC = 7. _____
   Dry out

8. CHACNTMET = 8. _____
   Device for collecting rain water

9. TSBSO = 9. _____
   Stakes

10. LDNEREUVA = 10. _____
    Took apart the strands of rope or yarn

11. IEERE = 11. _____
    Unnerving or unusual in a way that suggests a connection with the supernatural

12. NVEHADSI = 12. _____
    Disappeared

13. GNLLIAIF = 13. _____
    Thrashing or moving violently or uncontrollably

14. LAAAIRM = 14. _____
    Recurring illness common in hot countries, characterized by chills & fever

15. LRAWEED = 15. _____
    Away from the wind

The Cay Vocabulary Jugle Letters 4 Answer Key

1. EARF = 1. FARE
   Manage in doing something

2. RUGRNMMIU = 2. MURMURING
   Speaking softly

3. SEDKI = 3. DIKES
   Embankments to prevent flooding

4. NFREERIY = 4. REFINERY
   Place for processing raw materials such as oil or sugar

5. ILDTSELID = 5. DISTILLED
   Purified by boiling and condensing vapors

6. RTDEEHET = 6. TETHERED
   Tied to

7. RPAHC = 7. PARCH
   Dry out

8. CHACNTMET = 8. CATCHMENT
   Device for collecting rain water

9. TSBSO = 9. STOBS
   Stakes

10. LDNEREUVA =10. UNRAVELED
    Took apart the strands of rope or yarn

11. IEERE =11. EERIE
    Unnerving or unusual in a way that suggests a connection with the supernatural

12. NVEHADSI =12. VANISHED
    Disappeared

13. GNLLIAIF =13. FLAILING
    Thrashing or moving violently or uncontrollably

14. LAAAIRM =14. MALARIA
    Recurring illness common in hot countries, characterized by chills & fever

15. LRAWEED =15. LEEWARD
    Away from the wind

ALABASTER	Type of gypsum (white mineral) usually used for decorative plaster work
ANGUISH	Extreme anxiety
AWASH	Covered in water
CATCHMENT	Device for collecting rain water
CAY	Small, low island
CEASE	Stop

CELLOPHANE	Thin, transparent, waterproof material made from wood pulp
COARSER	Rougher
CREVICES	Narrow cracks
DEBRIS	Fragments of broken things
DIKES	Embankments to prevent flooding
DISTILLED	Purified by boiling and condensing vapors

DRONE	Low, humming sound
EBONY	Brownish-black color
EERIE	Unnerving or unusual in a way that suggests a connection with the supernatural
FARE	Manage in doing something
FLAILING	Thrashing or moving violently or uncontrollably
FRET	Worry

FRONDS	Large, divided leaves
GROPED	Searched by feeling
HONING	Sharpening
IDLING	Operating but not in gear
IRRITATING	Annoying; bothersome
LEEWARD	Away from the wind

LEGACY	Something handed down or left via will
MALARIA	Recurring illness common in hot countries, characterized by chills & fever
MURMURING	Speaking softly
MUTINY	Organized rebellion against ship's captain or another authority
NAVIGATION	Directing a vehicle's course
PARCH	Dry out

RECEDED	Went back or further away
REFINERY	Place for processing raw materials such as oil or sugar
SCOUR	Search carefully
SPAN	Extend over or across something
STOBS	Stakes
TETHERED	Tied to

TREACHEROUS	Involving hidden dangers
UNRAVELED	Took apart the strands of rope or yarn
VANISHED	Disappeared
VEILS	Like curtains
WELTED	Having ridges or bumps on the skin caused by being struck with something (like a whip)
WRENCHING	Pulling or twisting away

The Cay Vocabulary

CATCHMENT	COARSER	TETHERED	NAVIGATION	EBONY
STOBS	UNRAVELED	CREVICES	LEGACY	FRET
WELTED	HONING	FREE SPACE	MALARIA	SPAN
AWASH	CEASE	VEILS	MUTINY	RECEDED
FARE	IDLING	WRENCHING	CAY	VANISHED

The Cay Vocabulary

ALABASTER	FRONDS	GROPED	DRONE	IRRITATING
CELLOPHANE	DIKES	EERIE	PARCH	MURMURING
ANGUISH	DISTILLED	FREE SPACE	TREACHEROUS	SCOUR
LEEWARD	DEBRIS	VANISHED	CAY	WRENCHING
IDLING	FARE	RECEDED	MUTINY	VEILS

The Cay Vocabulary

WRENCHING	IRRITATING	SCOUR	STOBS	DEBRIS
IDLING	DRONE	FLAILING	DIKES	MALARIA
LEGACY	RECEDED	FREE SPACE	VEILS	NAVIGATION
MUTINY	FRONDS	CATCHMENT	TREACHEROUS	CEASE
EBONY	FARE	LEEWARD	CELLOPHANE	ALABASTER

The Cay Vocabulary

TETHERED	ANGUISH	GROPED	EERIE	WELTED
REFINERY	AWASH	SPAN	MURMURING	DISTILLED
CAY	PARCH	FREE SPACE	HONING	CREVICES
UNRAVELED	VANISHED	ALABASTER	CELLOPHANE	LEEWARD
FARE	EBONY	CEASE	TREACHEROUS	CATCHMENT

The Cay Vocabulary

FARE	DISTILLED	MURMURING	FRET	HONING
ANGUISH	IRRITATING	VEILS	SCOUR	CEASE
WRENCHING	LEEWARD	FREE SPACE	DEBRIS	IDLING
DRONE	CELLOPHANE	TETHERED	EERIE	EBONY
COARSER	FLAILING	TREACHEROUS	MALARIA	PARCH

The Cay Vocabulary

CATCHMENT	WELTED	GROPED	ALABASTER	FRONDS
CAY	LEGACY	DIKES	REFINERY	UNRAVELED
RECEDED	NAVIGATION	FREE SPACE	AWASH	SPAN
CREVICES	STOBS	PARCH	MALARIA	TREACHEROUS
FLAILING	COARSER	EBONY	EERIE	TETHERED

The Cay Vocabulary

SCOUR	EBONY	DIKES	PARCH	ANGUISH
CELLOPHANE	MUTINY	IRRITATING	HONING	FARE
TREACHEROUS	UNRAVELED	FREE SPACE	VEILS	ALABASTER
CAY	RECEDED	CEASE	DRONE	CATCHMENT
FLAILING	EERIE	WELTED	CREVICES	COARSER

The Cay Vocabulary

MURMURING	LEGACY	VANISHED	FRONDS	NAVIGATION
IDLING	LEEWARD	WRENCHING	SPAN	MALARIA
TETHERED	STOBS	FREE SPACE	DISTILLED	AWASH
REFINERY	GROPED	COARSER	CREVICES	WELTED
EERIE	FLAILING	CATCHMENT	DRONE	CEASE

The Cay Vocabulary

WRENCHING	CAY	STOBS	MUTINY	CEASE
MALARIA	DISTILLED	TETHERED	NAVIGATION	AWASH
VANISHED	FARE	FREE SPACE	CELLOPHANE	WELTED
FRONDS	HONING	UNRAVELED	MURMURING	CATCHMENT
ALABASTER	DEBRIS	COARSER	DRONE	FRET

The Cay Vocabulary

EERIE	GROPED	RECEDED	PARCH	CREVICES
SPAN	VEILS	IDLING	SCOUR	ANGUISH
LEEWARD	FLAILING	FREE SPACE	LEGACY	TREACHEROUS
EBONY	DIKES	FRET	DRONE	COARSER
DEBRIS	ALABASTER	CATCHMENT	MURMURING	UNRAVELED

The Cay Vocabulary

ANGUISH	TREACHEROUS	CEASE	CELLOPHANE	WELTED
MURMURING	WRENCHING	FRONDS	FARE	DRONE
DIKES	SPAN	FREE SPACE	ALABASTER	REFINERY
NAVIGATION	HONING	SCOUR	GROPED	IDLING
CREVICES	LEEWARD	EERIE	VANISHED	RECEDED

The Cay Vocabulary

PARCH	TETHERED	UNRAVELED	DISTILLED	MUTINY
EBONY	MALARIA	COARSER	CAY	DEBRIS
STOBS	IRRITATING	FREE SPACE	LEGACY	VEILS
FRET	AWASH	RECEDED	VANISHED	EERIE
LEEWARD	CREVICES	IDLING	GROPED	SCOUR

The Cay Vocabulary

UNRAVELED	PARCH	LEEWARD	WELTED	MALARIA
MURMURING	AWASH	DEBRIS	LEGACY	VEILS
NAVIGATION	FARE	FREE SPACE	GROPED	CAY
STOBS	CEASE	FRONDS	ALABASTER	DIKES
DISTILLED	IRRITATING	SPAN	EBONY	EERIE

The Cay Vocabulary

RECEDED	REFINERY	FLAILING	SCOUR	CELLOPHANE
HONING	VANISHED	MUTINY	CATCHMENT	DRONE
IDLING	ANGUISH	FREE SPACE	COARSER	TREACHEROUS
CREVICES	TETHERED	EERIE	EBONY	SPAN
IRRITATING	DISTILLED	DIKES	ALABASTER	FRONDS

The Cay Vocabulary

SPAN	VEILS	EERIE	PARCH	MALARIA
UNRAVELED	FRET	NAVIGATION	GROPED	WELTED
FARE	VANISHED	FREE SPACE	DIKES	FRONDS
DISTILLED	CELLOPHANE	SCOUR	AWASH	LEEWARD
MURMURING	REFINERY	HONING	RECEDED	DRONE

The Cay Vocabulary

IRRITATING	IDLING	CEASE	CATCHMENT	FLAILING
ANGUISH	STOBS	DEBRIS	CREVICES	EBONY
TREACHEROUS	WRENCHING	FREE SPACE	MUTINY	CAY
LEGACY	TETHERED	DRONE	RECEDED	HONING
REFINERY	MURMURING	LEEWARD	AWASH	SCOUR

The Cay Vocabulary

CEASE	IRRITATING	FRONDS	WRENCHING	NAVIGATION
PARCH	REFINERY	LEGACY	COARSER	CAY
IDLING	VANISHED	FREE SPACE	AWASH	FARE
TREACHEROUS	CREVICES	DRONE	ANGUISH	RECEDED
GROPED	HONING	WELTED	SPAN	CATCHMENT

The Cay Vocabulary

DEBRIS	MURMURING	CELLOPHANE	VEILS	UNRAVELED
TETHERED	DISTILLED	EBONY	STOBS	DIKES
MUTINY	MALARIA	FREE SPACE	ALABASTER	LEEWARD
FLAILING	FRET	CATCHMENT	SPAN	WELTED
HONING	GROPED	RECEDED	ANGUISH	DRONE

The Cay Vocabulary

CELLOPHANE	DIKES	DEBRIS	LEEWARD	IRRITATING
STOBS	MUTINY	TETHERED	SPAN	RECEDED
CAY	DRONE	FREE SPACE	EBONY	EERIE
WELTED	FLAILING	AWASH	HONING	REFINERY
FRONDS	MURMURING	PARCH	COARSER	ALABASTER

The Cay Vocabulary

FARE	WRENCHING	IDLING	VEILS	VANISHED
GROPED	MALARIA	DISTILLED	CREVICES	ANGUISH
UNRAVELED	NAVIGATION	FREE SPACE	CATCHMENT	SCOUR
FRET	CEASE	ALABASTER	COARSER	PARCH
MURMURING	FRONDS	REFINERY	HONING	AWASH

The Cay Vocabulary

LEGACY	RECEDED	MALARIA	SCOUR	VANISHED
DEBRIS	COARSER	UNRAVELED	MURMURING	REFINERY
EBONY	DISTILLED	FREE SPACE	CAY	WRENCHING
AWASH	LEEWARD	CREVICES	FRET	IDLING
HONING	DIKES	TETHERED	ALABASTER	NAVIGATION

The Cay Vocabulary

CATCHMENT	DRONE	GROPED	EERIE	VEILS
FARE	CEASE	WELTED	TREACHEROUS	ANGUISH
SPAN	MUTINY	FREE SPACE	IRRITATING	CELLOPHANE
FLAILING	FRONDS	NAVIGATION	ALABASTER	TETHERED
DIKES	HONING	IDLING	FRET	CREVICES

The Cay Vocabulary

REFINERY	CAY	TREACHEROUS	MUTINY	MALARIA
NAVIGATION	WRENCHING	VEILS	DISTILLED	FARE
TETHERED	ALABASTER	FREE SPACE	IDLING	AWASH
LEEWARD	ANGUISH	CEASE	LEGACY	CATCHMENT
GROPED	DIKES	HONING	FLAILING	CREVICES

The Cay Vocabulary

SPAN	STOBS	DEBRIS	FRET	EBONY
EERIE	FRONDS	DRONE	COARSER	IRRITATING
VANISHED	RECEDED	FREE SPACE	SCOUR	CELLOPHANE
PARCH	MURMURING	CREVICES	FLAILING	HONING
DIKES	GROPED	CATCHMENT	LEGACY	CEASE

The Cay Vocabulary

FARE	MALARIA	IDLING	DRONE	NAVIGATION
TETHERED	LEGACY	LEEWARD	VEILS	PARCH
UNRAVELED	GROPED	FREE SPACE	CREVICES	CELLOPHANE
COARSER	EERIE	DEBRIS	AWASH	MURMURING
IRRITATING	HONING	REFINERY	SPAN	DIKES

The Cay Vocabulary

ALABASTER	CATCHMENT	FRONDS	STOBS	MUTINY
DISTILLED	TREACHEROUS	EBONY	CAY	CEASE
SCOUR	FRET	FREE SPACE	RECEDED	ANGUISH
WRENCHING	FLAILING	DIKES	SPAN	REFINERY
HONING	IRRITATING	MURMURING	AWASH	DEBRIS

The Cay Vocabulary

RECEDED	COARSER	NAVIGATION	SPAN	FRONDS
EBONY	ALABASTER	PARCH	CATCHMENT	ANGUISH
REFINERY	IRRITATING	FREE SPACE	IDLING	MALARIA
MURMURING	WELTED	DISTILLED	EERIE	DRONE
WRENCHING	FLAILING	GROPED	TREACHEROUS	FRET

The Cay Vocabulary

DIKES	LEEWARD	MUTINY	AWASH	CEASE
HONING	SCOUR	DEBRIS	VEILS	CAY
FARE	TETHERED	FREE SPACE	LEGACY	VANISHED
CREVICES	CELLOPHANE	FRET	TREACHEROUS	GROPED
FLAILING	WRENCHING	DRONE	EERIE	DISTILLED

The Cay Vocabulary

PARCH	CAY	UNRAVELED	CATCHMENT	FRONDS
LEEWARD	DISTILLED	REFINERY	ALABASTER	ANGUISH
EERIE	IRRITATING	FREE SPACE	GROPED	AWASH
SPAN	TREACHEROUS	WELTED	CEASE	LEGACY
DRONE	VEILS	MUTINY	CELLOPHANE	FLAILING

The Cay Vocabulary

CREVICES	DIKES	TETHERED	MALARIA	NAVIGATION
MURMURING	COARSER	VANISHED	FARE	EBONY
RECEDED	IDLING	FREE SPACE	DEBRIS	FRET
WRENCHING	SCOUR	FLAILING	CELLOPHANE	MUTINY
VEILS	DRONE	LEGACY	CEASE	WELTED

The Cay Vocabulary

ALABASTER	AWASH	VEILS	VANISHED	FARE
MUTINY	COARSER	STOBS	RECEDED	TREACHEROUS
GROPED	EBONY	FREE SPACE	DISTILLED	LEEWARD
FLAILING	REFINERY	CELLOPHANE	LEGACY	FRET
CEASE	EERIE	CAY	SCOUR	IDLING

The Cay Vocabulary

CREVICES	NAVIGATION	WRENCHING	PARCH	HONING
WELTED	ANGUISH	MURMURING	FRONDS	MALARIA
DIKES	DRONE	FREE SPACE	SPAN	UNRAVELED
CATCHMENT	TETHERED	IDLING	SCOUR	CAY
EERIE	CEASE	FRET	LEGACY	CELLOPHANE

www.ingramcontent.com/pod-product-compliance
Lightning Source LLC
Chambersburg PA
CBHW081457070526
44586CB00019B/2400